SIGNS OF TIME

An Introduction to Mesoamerican Astrology

by Bruce Scofield

One Reed Publications

Copyright: (C) 1994 by Bruce Scofield

Published by : One Reed Publications
PO Box 561
Amherst, MA 01004-0561

Printed in the United States of America.

First Edition
First Printing 1994.

Library of Congress Catalog Card Number: 94-067580
ISBN 0-9628031-1-1

Some of the text in this book has been adapted from articles written by
the author that were published in *Considerations* (Vol.III:1,2,3:1985),
Welcome to Planet Earth (Vol.10:4:1990),*National Council for
Geocosmic Research Journal* (1991), and *Dell Horoscope* (Sept. 1994).

Cover illustration: Quetzalcoatl descending from the sky on a rope ladder
between symbols of Moon, Sun and Venus. He stands over Tenochtitlan,
capital city of the Aztecs. The 20 day-signs frame the scene.

Additional copies of this book, and also its companion book *Day Signs:
Native American Astrology From Ancient Mexico,* may be ordered
directly from the publisher. When ordering, enclose $13.50 for each book
(either title - includes P & H).

Table of Contents

Forward

Astrology has played a very important role in the early development of every major civilization. In the case of the Western world, astrology was at the cutting edge of knowledge for millennia beginning with ancient Mesopotamian civilization and continuing through the Renaissance. The scientists of those times were astrologers and many of their names and some of their works have come down to us. It was not until the 17th century that several historical developments, including the rise of fundamentalist Christianity, scientific materialism and the insurance business caused the subject to lose its former high status. In the 20th century a revival of astrology began and the subject expanded to accommodate the interest in human psychology that characterized the modern period.

As modern Western astrology moves toward respectability, it is important that it be re-established on the firmest foundation, one that can tolerate the biased criticism and blind arrogance of uninformed scientists and preachers. An important step in this process lies in a study of astrology's roots, how it came into being and for what reasons.

The indigenous astrology of ancient Mesoamerica provides us with a unique opportunity to study astrology in one of its early forms. Ancient Mesopotamia, where the roots of Western astrology lie, is four or five thousand years distant and barely discernible. The astrological texts of Roman times, the few that still exist, are records of a mature astrology developed for the analysis and understanding of both nations and individuals. These late classical texts stand on 2-3,000 years of astrological development in the Near East.[1] In comparison, the astrology of the Maya and Aztecs was developed to a similar level as that of ancient Mesopotamia, and most of it thrived until only five hundred years ago. Some survives today. This book is an attempt to piece together the various strands of this truly Native American astrology from pre-Columbian, colonial and current ethnographic sources, and to present it as a body of knowledge in a format which can be used by today's astrologers and students of astrology.

The civilizations of the Maya and Aztec have always held a special fascination for Westerners. Not only their sacrificial rituals and apparent primitivism, but also their amazing architectural and intellectually dazzling astronomical accomplishments have stirred imaginations. In the 1970's Eric Von Danniken published a series of books, the first titled *Chariots of the Gods,* in which he suggested that visitors from outer space were connected with Mayan civilization, its temples and pyramids. A convicted forger, Von Danniken captured the public's interest with his thesis which was unsubstantiated and largely contrived, not to mention obliquely racist. The scientific community, which has replaced the Church as the institution most responsible for defining reality to the public, responded to Von Danniken by presenting a more sober view of the achievements of these ancient civilizations in a number of books and documentaries. Since then there has been an outpouring of academic research on the subject, including popular works, college textbooks and anthologies of collected papers. What the academics are currently discovering has been known all along by serious researchers, that *Mesoamerican astronomy existed to support Mesoamerican astrology.* Astrology was the real interest of these ancient peoples.

While the astronomy of ancient Mesoamerica has been researched intensely, the astrology has been avoided or ignored. Among the academic community, the notion does not yet exist that astrology could actually work and therefore be worthy of study.[2] Still, the astronomers and archaeologists have contributed greatly to our understanding of ancient science. Their writings contain all the facts one would want to know about the great achievements of the Maya, their vigesimal mathematics, their accurate computations of astronomical cycles, and their elaborate tables of planetary and calendar positions. Because so much has already been written about the astronomy of ancient Mesoamerica, I have chosen to bypass this material except where it is appropriate to the study. Interested readers who wish to further explore the purely astronomical side of the subject might begin with the writings of Anthony Aveni.

In writing this book I have tried to steer a course through the material that lies somewhere between the solid (though limiting) groundwork of the materialistic academic mind, and the realm of possibilities open to those who practice astrology. Some readers may find my approach to the subject matter as unimaginative; others may find it refreshing to not be bombarded with unsubstantiated assumptions in pseudo-academic disguise. There are no extreme stretches of the imagination in this book, such as are found in the writings of Jose Arguelles or Frank Waters. I attempt instead to explain what is verifiably known about Mesoamerican astrology and how it might be used today. I have also kept comparisons with other systems to a minimum, allowing readers the opportunity to learn the material on its own terms and make their own connections. This is a guidebook to Mesoamerican astrology, not an argument for my own thesis about what it means and how it should be used.

The subject of Mesoamerican astrology is far more complex than one would suspect, given the limited number of sources both historic and current. I have consequently narrowed the field of investigation to those aspects of the native astrology that were the most important or the most widely practiced. Hopefully, the material presented here will stimulate interest in the subject and eventually lead to its rehabilitation in some form.

Readers who find the brief delineations of the day-signs in this book intriguing should look to the companion book *Day-Signs: Native American Astrology From Ancient Mexico* for longer and deeper interpretations of the signs and their influence on personality.

The pronounuciation of Maya and Nauhuatl (Aztec) words may present problems for English speakers. In general, the words are pronounced as they are spelled in Spanish. For example, Nahuatl, which is the name of the language group that the Aztecs were a part of, is pronounced Nah-wahtl. The "tl" ending is common in this language and is not actually a separate sylable. It hangs at the end of the sylable and is sounded something like the ending of the word "battle." In general, Nahuatl words have the accent on the next-to-last syllable. Maya words, on the other hand, are usually accented on the last syllable, but they are also pronounced as they are spelled in Spanish. One exception is the "x" which is pronounced as in old Spanish, as an "sh." Below are some common words and names with approximate English pronounciation.

Quetzalcoat: Ket-zal-*koe*-atl
Tezcatlipoca: Tez-cat-lee-*poe*-ka
Chalchihuitlicue: Chal-chi-whit-lee-*ku*-ee
Xolotl: *Show*-lotl
tonalamatl: toe-nahl-*ah*-mahtl
tonalpouhalli: toe-nahl-poe-*whal*-lee
tonalli: toe-*nah*-lee
Tenochtitlan: Ten-oach-*teet*-lahn
Teotihuacan: Tay-oh-tee-*wah*-cahn
Palenque: Pah-len-*kay*
Chichen Itza: Chee-*chen* Eet-*zuh*
Uxmal: Ush-*mahl*
Imix: ee-*mish*
Ahau: Ah-*haw*
katun: kah-*tune*
tzolkin: zole-*keen*
uinal: wee-*nahl*
kin: keen

I would like to thank the follow individuals for their help and support. Barry Orr's computer programming allowed for rapid and accurate calculations of the various cycles used by Mesoamerican astrologers. The results of his efforts are available in the computer program Aztec/Maya Astro-Report. Daisy Orr's close observations of current trends and their relationship to the day- signs and trecena have stimulated my thinking on the subject considerably, as has correspondence from Ray Kerkhove in Australia and Hugo Carrano in Mexico. Robert Zoller and the late A.H. Blackwell read an early version of the manuscript and made many useful suggestions. John Major Jenkins spotted some typos and numerical errors thus improving the accuracy of the data. Thanks also to Valerie Vaughan for her help with library research and for proofreading the manuscript. Finally, I wish to thank my mother, Lucy Scofield, for her support of my publishing interests. The printing of the book itself was made possible through her generosity.

Section I

Mesoamerican Astrology Explained

"The evidence strongly indicates that the real purpose of Maya calendrical astronomy was to place man and historical events in harmonious context within the endless cycles of celestial bodies and of time itself. Astronomical knowledge and calendrical arithmetic were used for astrological divinations of the future. By understanding the patterns in planetary motions, the calendar priest-astronomers could predict future configurations and arrange for the propitious timing of rituals." John B. Carlson [1981:206]

"[Maya] Ritual, war, trade, marriage, accession, and other social activities were more likely to succeed if they were conducted at the proper place and time. Specialists in the complex patterns of time and in the movements of the heavens, like Western astrologers, kept track of the movements of the stars and planets to discover when it was favorable to proceed. As the Maya exploited the patterns of power in time and space, they used ritual to control the dangerous and powerful energies they released." Linda Schele and David Friedel [1990:73]

"Regardless of identification, the pictures of star groups in the codices emphasize the use of celestial bodies to indicate both time and direction. They also suggest a strong connection between astrology and astronomy. Celestial events are constantly linked to the rise and fall of various rulers, battles fought, and great disasters which occurred." Anthony Aveni [1980:38]

"The high hopes entertained for decisive results from a strictly astronomical approach [to Maya inscriptions] have not been fullfilled. I think that is because the Maya priests did not use astronomy as an exact science. Instead, they fashioned it to their mystical and poetical approach. Associations of celestial phenomena with lucky or unlucky days, or connections deep in mythology were, I am sure, of more importance than an exact record of when they occurred. Since these are the methods of the astrologer rather than of the astronomer, the precise technique of the latter is often of little value in augmenting knowledge of the meaning of the inscriptions."
J. Eric S.Thompson [1960:33]

Chapter 1

The Prehistoric Origins of Astrology

Early humans lived in the largely unconscious world of the animal kingdom. They were a part of the ecosystem, occupying a particular niche in the scheme of life and directly dependent on the rest of nature for their very survival. The cyclic changing of the seasons, the renewal of vegetation, and the migration of animals were survival realities that could be correlated with the movements of the Sun, which was the most awesome feature of the sacred and life-giving world in which these humans lived.

The facts of the diurnal experience of light and dark, day and night, create an all-pervasive polarity that establishes a foundation for behavior and routine. It is the Sun that awakens us at dawn and ushers in a time of order and clarity. The night is mysterious and dangerous, a time of confusion. The polarities of light and dark, male and female, and above and below also create a texture to awareness. Circadian cycles, the daily biological rhythms that regulate the growth and development of cells and higher life forms, appear to utilize this consistent recurring pattern of light and dark.[1] It may be that life itself, in evolving all the various pulses and rhythms which make growth and adaptation possible, latched onto this alternating pattern as a model. If this be the case, then there may be a very old and profound biological basis for astrology.

The Sun sustains life on our planet. Plants grow toward the Sun, animals eat the plants, and humans eat both. As agriculture developed this "solar primacy" was recognized. The movements of the Sun and the corresponding seasonal turn of life, death, and renewal created a sense of cyclic time to early humans. They perceived time as a repetition of cycles, not a linear movement from past to present, and also as a force that regulated their lives. From this perspective time can be observed in every aspect of the changing sky. The time of sunrise and the time of sunset delineate a fundamental unit of time -- the day itself. The cycle of the year, which correlates with the positions on the horizon where the Sun rises and sets, gave early humans a further sense of order as they emerged into a more conscious and less instinctive experience of life.

Early humans connected night sounds, the magic of the dream world and erotic moods with the Moon. The Moon became linked with tides, both inner and outer, with biological cycles, particularly fertility cycles, and also with the behaviors of animals. Societies that kept domesticated herds were undoubtedly cognizant of such things and made efforts to observe the Moon and record its cycle. Hesiod's Works and Days, one of the earliest pieces of writing in the Western world, does exactly this.

Astrology is the study and knowledge of man's relationship to the Sun, Moon, the planets and stars. In any period of history or pre-history the type of astrology used characterizes the type and quality of human response to life in general. As humans developed more complex social structures, the regular and predictable movements of the Sun, Moon and planets became the model for social order. The order in the heavens suggested a pattern to re-create on earth. To secure predictability, the heavenly order was to be duplicated in the social order.

Astrology, astronomy and calendar science started out as the same endeavor; a way of gaining some measure of control over the constantly changing environment. Close, methodical observation of the heavenly bodies requires at least three things: a person who will do the watching, a consistently used observation station or device, and a means of recording and transmitting the data. The gnomon, simply a stick placed in the ground around which shadow patterns are noted, was probably the first scientific instrument. Later, more complex, multi-function observatories were built.   These temple/observatories were both centers of ritual and worship, and measuring and recording devices.

The Sun rises in the east, but its actual position on the eastern horizon varies during the year. During the winter it rises to the south of the true east point, and during the summer it rises to the north (see

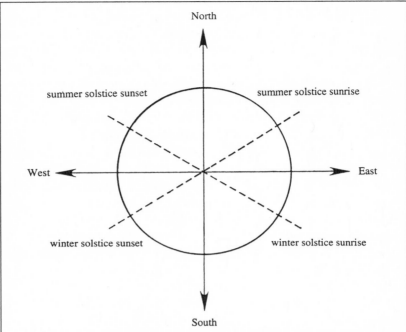

Figure 1. The four directions are established by the rising and setting positions of the Sun. The Sun rises due east and sets due west on the first day of spring (vernal equinox) and the first day of autumn (autumnal equinox). North and south lie at the midpoint of the summer and winter solstice sunrise and sunset points.

Figure 1.). The extreme south/east and north/east rising positions were carefully noted by ancient skywatchers. When rising near these extremes, the Sun's movement is very slow, so slow that these positions have come to be known as the solstices, literally, the Sun stand-still points. After a few days of hardly detectable movement, the rising or setting Sun reverses its direction and begins to move toward its other extreme which it reaches in six months. The midpoint of this movement is the equinox which we observe as the first day of spring or fall. At the equinoxes the length of daylight and darkness are equal, and sunrise and sunset define the perfect east-west direction. Once an east-west line is established, alignment on earth with the reality of the sky is possible. In a sense, the locating, naming and utilization of the four direction is an astrological act, an act of patterning the cosmic order, of bringing heaven to earth.

The knowledge based on observation of the rising positions of the Sun was used for agriculture. The link between the Sun and vegetation is indeed an obvious one. Growing dates, dates of last frost, harvest dates, times of weather and seasonal changes, etc. become predictable with knowledge of the Sun's movements. As soon as horizon positions of the Sun become recognized and marked off with reference to specific horizon features or special stone and building alignments, a science of prediction is possible. The Sun's movements define the directions, which allows for astronomically-oriented architectural construction.

The locating of the four directions is common to most early cultures. By defining the space around us, we become the center of the microcosm. The east, the direction of the emerging Sun (or god), is frequently regarded as the principal direction, the direction to face towards. Life begins in the east. The word "orientation" which has come to mean becoming organized in space, literally means "facing east." West, where the Sun sets, is the entrance to the underworld (the dying Sun), north is to your left and south to the right. The meanings assigned to the four directions are remarkably similar throughout the world. This tradition survives in Western astrology as the four elements, in Christianity as the four evangelists and in the Tarot as the four suits.

The act of using the sky to bring order to the world of humanity, which in this case means locating the four directions, is both an astrological and magical process. Among the ancients, the newly created space became sacred, and markers (often stones) were set up to make the orientation permanent. Examples of this are Stonehenge and the pyramids of Egypt and Mexico. Additional astronomically determined lines (eg. lunar, planetary and stellar rises and sets) were often incorporated into these structures, further extending the alignment of the human world with the logic of the sky. The beginnings of civilization as we know it occurred when the dwellers in the microcosm, humans, imitated the macrocosm seen in the sky.[2]

The movements of the Moon are more astronomically complex and therefore more mysterious. The Moon does not rise or set at the same time every solar day, and its visible form changes through the course of its full cycle. Watchers of the Moon were primarily concerned with its correlation to fertility cycles and feeding patterns.[3] Knowledge of breeding times and lengths of gestation in mammals were aided by Moon-watching. The changing of tides has always been associated with the movements of the Moon. It has long been known that the highest tides coincide with the new and full Moons. The full Moon itself was regarded as a force that brought out altered behaviors in humans, as it still appears to do.

The movements of both the Sun and the Moon offer two different means of keeping time and creating a sense of order in daily life. The Moon was used for short term time-keeping. North American Indians, for example, would count the number of "Moons" between events. Besides short-term day-counting, the Sun is used for longer time-keeping purposes of a year or more. Because the Moon's cycle (the month) and that of the Sun (the year) are not cleanly reconciled with each other, many early cultures struggled to find a compromise between these two kinds of time. Their solutions were often quite complex, even highly sophisticated in some cases.[4]

Astrology developed out of an awareness that man is an integral part of nature and is dependent upon it for survival. As has been suggested, in very early times, the Sun was seen as the giver of life and the Moon as the mysterious link with the sea and reproduction. Astrology at this level was simply a set of instinctively perceived connections between the sky and the parts of one vast ecosystem. The Sun and Moon both offered a sense of time and space, as well as a sense of sequence and history. The measurement and close observation of the Sun and Moon marked a new stage of astrology, a stage where man was actually developing a technology of control. Specialists, the first astro-scientists, emerged to do the work and transmit it to others. Knowledge of the Sun's movements help create plant agriculture while knowledge of the Moon's cycles did the same for hunting and animal husbandry and hunting. Astrology became the study and interpretation of the correlations between the heavens and biological life on earth. In contrast to the chaos of human life, the sky is more or less constant, ordered and ultimately predictable. It made good sense to follow the sky and build on the links with life on earth that were already apparent.

A chronology of archaeoastrology will help to put the subject matter of this book in better perspective. While astrology is an activity that man has been engaged in since very early times, its level of sophistication is relative to the developmental level of the society that uses it. Using the terminology of anthropology in a very generalized way, the Paleolithic stage in pre-history was characterized by the following: small groups of between 20 to 60 persons, migration to and from fixed places of habitation such as caves, dependence on migrating herds and seasonal plants for food, primitive tools and implements. At this cultural level astrology may have consisted in simply recognizing the signs that aided in the totally consuming occupation of survival. These are the simple movements of the Sun and Moon as described above.

The invention of agriculture and domestication of animals led to the Neolithic stage. On this level, humans no longer needed to migrate with the food supply, they kept it where they wanted it. Women became more valued because they were normally the ones who nurtured the food supply. Pottery, weaving and house-building became established practices. Astrology at this stage consisted of locating the four directions, creating sacred space, and developing a calendar and rituals that punctuated the year. The fragility of the group was recognized, cohesive community became paramount and security became linked to the regularity of the sky. The importance of the Sun, because it kept the crops growing, inspired and stimulated ritual activities designed to keep the Sun on its regular path. There appears to have been a deep fear that the order which had been created might be lost. The magical idea that man can act on the cosmos, and not just be acted upon, became a part of religious ritual. Certain individuals in the group would take on the responsibility of watching the sky and locating crucial points in time. Over the centuries an oral tradition of sky lore and sky prognostication developed and was passed on. The names and symbolism given to regions of the sky acquired a kind of permanence in the collective mind. On this Neolithic cultural level are found a number of groups which still survive, with some adaptations, to this day, including the Pueblo Indian culture of the American Southwest. In many respects, they practiced and still do, to some extent, a kind of Neolithic astrology.

The next major stage in the evolution of culture might be called the City State. The great challenge humans faced in reaching this level of cultural development was how to bring a large number of different social classes together in an orderly manner. Again, the orderliness of the sky was both the model and the solution. To implement this solution full-time interpreters of the sky, an astronomical priesthood, were needed. At certain times in many cultures the power of this group rivaled that of the chief warrior, the king. Sky watching and interpreting became more complex and sophisticated. Elaborate temple/observatories were constructed to facilitate the interaction between humans and the sky. The fundamental issues of existence, as expressed in culture myths and symbols, gradually came to be associated (only after generations of observations) with specific stars and planets. The city itself was seen as an embodiment of heaven on earth, the cosmic order brought down to the world of man. The notion that the laws governing the sky and heavenly bodies should be the same for man led to greater control over the population by a few sky- watchers/priests.

The cities and the culture centers of ancient Egypt and Mesopotamia are good examples of the cultural stage of the City State. It was out of these societies that our own Western astrology was born. However, today we stand roughly 4,000 to 5,000 years distant from these peoples and no longer have clear ideas of what their astrology was really like. In many ways we have lost our oldest astrological roots.

Such is not the case for the cultures of Mesoamerica. In the early 16th century the Spanish conquistadors came upon a culture that was at about the same level of cultural development as the ancient Egyptians and Mesopotamians. Writing had not become fully developed, and much importance was still placed on the oral tradition. The shamanic origins of religion were still close to the surface. Thanks in part to the slash and burn tactics of the conquistadors and the religious zeal of the friars, the loss of information about the traditional astrology of Mesoamerica is staggering, but we are still in an excellent position to learn about an archaic form of astrology from what is left. Such an attempt is made in the following chapters.

Chapter 2

Introduction to Mesoamerica

In the region known today as Mexico and northern Central America there developed in pre-Columbian times an astrological divination system that was perpetuated by successive cultures for perhaps 2,000 years. The ancient Mesoamericans were avid skywatchers who perceived a host of linkages between periods of time, the movements of the heavenly bodies, and life on earth. They integrated the order they perceived in the sky into their ceremonial centers, their social structure, and even into the lives of individuals. This fusion of man and sky was also developed elsewhere at earlier times (eg. ancient China and Mesopotamia), but the cultures of Mesoamerica grew in isolation from the rest of the world, and at a later date. This book attempts to piece together the various components of ancient Mesoamerican astrology, which, like that of the ancient Old World civilizations, was deeply integrated and inseparable from astronomy, calendrics, mythology, religion, philosophical thought, and social organization.

History

Ancient Mesoamerican culture evolved in the area ranging from about 23 degrees north latitude in Mexico to the south as far as what is now called El Salvador and western Honduras. (See Figure 2.) Village life and pottery began to apear in this region around -2500, but it wasn't until about -1500 that organized centers developed in the Gulf Coast region. Between -1000 and +50 large cultural and religious centers apeared around the Gulf Coast and also in the Oaxacan highlands. It was from these centers that the basic forms for social organization and religion were established, and these would influence the entire Mesoamerican region for centuries.

The early peoples of the Gulf Coast region have come to be known as the Olmecs -- not their real name but one given to them long after they had disapeared. They built huge pyramids and monuments, some of which can be seen today at the archaeological sites of Tres Zapotes, San Lorenzo, and La Venta. The Olmec were also outstanding artists whose works were carried by traders throughout Mexico and Central America. Their ideas on religion no doubt spread as widely. On some of their monuments are inscriptions which appear to be early depictions of some of the most important gods in Mesoamerica. Contemporary with the Olmec cultures along the Gulf Coast, a ceremonial center was developed on a broad, flat mountaintop near present day Oaxaca. Elaborate stone carvings and other evidence of a major leap forward in culture are found there at Monte Alban. In the archaeological remains of both the Olmec and Monte Alban cultures are evidence of hieroglyphic writing and the use of the 260-day divinatory calendar. The historical period which includes these cultures has been named by archaeologists the Formative or Pre-Classic.

As Olmec civilization declined in the Gulf Coast area, other centers were springing up elsewhere. At Teotihuacan, just northeast of modern-day Mexico City, the enormous pyramids of the Sun and Moon were constructed along a roadway several miles long. Here, the earliest phase of what was perhaps Mesoamerica's largest ceremonial center and city began around 100 BC. A well planned center, Teotihuacan expanded, reaching a peak around the 4th or 5th centuries AD. By +300 other major centers were emerging in the valley of Mexico, the region near present day Oaxaca, and in the Guatamalan jungles. Over the following 600 years, a tremendous flowering of culture occurred in these and other areas. This historical period, known as the Classic, was the time when the finest sculpture, art work, astronomy and picture writing was produced in Mesoamerica. The Maya, with their centers of Tikal, Copan, and Palenque, developed what was probably the most sophisticated astronomy and writing systems in Mesoamerica. At Monte Alban, the Zapotecs built up and extended the original mountain top ceremonial center, adding   numerous platforms for temples,

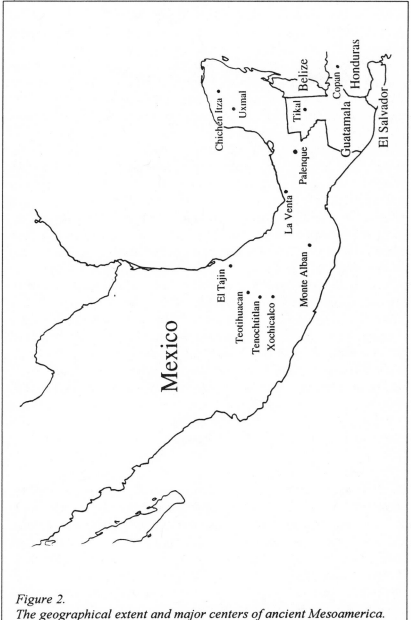

Figure 2.
The geographical extent and major centers of ancient Mesoamerica.

ballcourts, and what was probably an observatory.   While Europe was in the dark ages, Mesoamerica was throbbing with creative energy.

Teotihuacan mysteriously collapsed around +750, probably sacked by invading warrior tribes from the north. The Mayan centers to the south and Monte Alban to the southwest suffered a similar decline about 150 years later. The cause of this turn away from high civilization is still being debated by historians and archaeologists.[1]

The Post-Classic period (usually dated from about +900 on) was a time of changes and reorganization in Mesoamerica. During this period the Toltecs from their city Tollan, now the archaeological site of Tula north of Mexico City, forged an empire that eventually influenced a large part of Mesoamerica, including the Mayan city Chichen Itza in the Yucatan region. There the Maya reorganized several of their centers into what was called the league of Mayapan, a unification that lasted for only a few centuries. By the time of the arrival of the Spaniards, the Maya had once again deserted their ceremonial centers and had returned to life in small villages. In the valley of Mexico, however, the Aztecs were at the height of empire. The semi-nomadic Aztecs had wandered into the valley of Mexico in the 14th century and rapidly conquered their neighbors.[2]   They claimed Toltec descent, as did aspiring empire builders at that time, and became the main carriers of the surviving Classic Mesoamerican culture.

The Sources

Our knowledge of ancient Mesoamerican astrology is based on a few surviving relics, reports from the Spanish conquerors, and the living oral traditions.   Unfortunately, the Spanish friars burned thousands (nearly all) of the Maya and Aztec picture books, believing them to be the works of the devil.[3] Despite the massive losses, a handful of pre-Conquest manuscripts are still in existence. Because the Aztecs were flourishing at the time of the conquest, some material from their empire survived. It is from this collection that much of our knowledge of traditional Mesoamerican astrology and astronomy comes. It is fortunate for us that, in their astronomy and astrology, the Aztecs were perpetuating a much older tradition. Much of what they and their neighbors practiced was parallel (though cruder in some ways) to earlier Maya, Toltec, or other Mesoamerican systems. The major differences are in regard to the names of the gods which play such an important role in delineating the nature of the various aspects of the Aztec astrological-divinatory system. In this book I will draw from both Aztec era and the earlier Maya sources, using primary references wherever possible.

Most of the pre-Columbian picture books, known as codices, contain either astronomical or historical information. The four known Mayan codices, painted on a paper made from bark, contain tables of Venus positions, tables of eclipses, and other astronomical and calendar-related matters.[4] These codices also contain astrological material in the form of a divinatory almanac listing favorable and unfavorable days for various activities. A group of Mexican pre-conquest codices, called the Borgia group, contain depictions of the sequence of days and their ruling gods in the 260-day divinatory and astrological calendar. These picture books, painted on animal skins, were probably from the Mixtec area of Mexico, not from the Aztec capital itself. Assuming that the few surviving books constitute a fair sampling of pre-Coquest writings, the fact that so many of them are about the sky and calendar rhythms is evidence that these cultures were very serious about such matters.

Other useful sources include the writings of the Spanish friars. The Florentine Codex, the writings of Bernardino de Sahagún, is perhaps the most important. Sahagún, who arrived in Mexico in 1529, just eight years after the conquest, actually prepared a questionnaire with which to gather information about the natives. He collected and copied texts and spoke with elders whenever possible so that he would fully understand the ancient doctrines. He kept this project going for fifty years, the result being what is called the Florentine Codex, a history of ancient Mexico and its customs. One section of this work deals with astrology and the soothsayers of pre-conquest Mexico.

Like Sahagún, Diego Durán also wrote about Aztec matters, though it was years after the conquest that he recorded some material on the sacred calendar and its fates. Diego de Landa's book, *Relacion de las Cosas de Yucatan,* contains some information on the Maya calendar and even a note which attempts to link the Maya calendar with the European Julian calendar.[5] Sahagún, Durán and Landa were in some ways pioneer anthropologists, though their motive was to identify aspects of the culture that they were interested in eradicating. While their material on Mexican astrology is not deep (as one would expect), it does represent a large portion of what has been left to us.

After the Conquest, the Maya language was adapted to the Spanish alphabet.   Using this script, some of the traditional cosmology, astrology, and history was recorded in what has come to be known as the Books of Chilam Balam.   Chilam Balam, which means "jaguar-priest," was either a person who lived shortly before the arrival of the Spaniards or a general title for astrologer or prognosticator. The contents of the books are said to be transcriptions of material found in pre-conquest hieroglyphic manuscripts. There are several versions of these Books of Chilam Balam, each linked to a different town in Yucatan, though each is basically similar. Because these books were written well after the Conquest, parts of them contain a mixture of both native and Spanish ideas about the calendar and astrology.   For example, in the Codex Perez and the Book of Chilam Balam of Mani are found descriptions of the twelve Western zodiac signs next to a listing of good and bad days in the Maya astrological calendar.

The Cosmos and The Gods

The gods of Mesoamerica, like gods from other ancient cultures, were personifications of powerful forces that affect the lives of men, projections of the inner life of man, and in some cases, deified tribal leaders of ancient times.   Throughout the world one finds that rain deities are prominent in agricultural societies, while among hunters, warrior gods stand out.   In the case of the Aztecs, a balance was achieved between a tribal war god and the chief rain god of the farmers, both of them sharing the same temple.   As in the Old World cultures, the gods were assigned rulership over specific aspects of the universe as it was conceived.   In order to understand the distinctions of rulership in the astrological-divinatory system, one must first understand the distinctions among the major deities.

Individual Mesoamerican gods were often perceived as having several manifestations. Frequently there were four principle forms for a god. Each aspect of the god would be linked to one of the four directions, sharing its symbolism and color. Many gods were a duality; male and female components being equal. Mesoamerican gods are characterized by animal-like features or associations. The serpent and the jaguar in particular were well represented in both the Aztec and Maya god systems.

The Maya and the Aztec pantheons were similar in basic structure. At the top of the hierarchy of gods, living in the highest of thirteen heavens, was an old creator god, Hunab Ku to the Maya. This god was remote from the world; the creation had long ago been accomplished and his immediate presence was not vital to human life. For the Aztecs, this god was a duality; Ometecuhtli the supreme lord-creator and his female counterpart, or other half, Omecihuatl. Another name for this same god-duality was Tonacatecuhtli and Tonacacihuatl. After the imposition of missionary activity it was the male side of this creator pair that was usually associated with the Christian god.

Beneath this supreme, though remote, level of deity were the various nature and warrior deities. Probably among the oldest of the Mesoamerican gods were those associated with nature and rain, the gods of the peasants and farmers. Chac, the principal rain god of the Maya, had four aspects, one for each of the cardinal points. His face with its long nose is found sculpted on temple walls throughout Yucatan where rain is not so abundant. In the valley of Mexico, Tlaloc was Chac's counterpart. Tlaloc presided over a number of water deities including the Tlalocs, who were like fairies, and Chalchihuitlicue, the goddess of sudden storms. Another class of nature deity were the various gods of corn. The Aztecs had several manifestations of the corn god, each representing a particular aspect of the growth cycle.

There were a smaller number of important female deities, many of them linked to vegetation and the Moon. The Maya goddess Ixchel was the goddess of floods, pregnancy, the Moon and weaving. She was personified as an angry old woman, with a serpent in her hand

and crossbows on her skirt, fully capable of destroying the world with a flood. Ixchel's counterpart among the Aztecs was Chachihuitlicue, the Lady of the Jade Skirt and controller of sudden disastrous storms. Another important Aztec goddess was Tlazolteol, a goddess who heard confessions and was known as the Eater of Filth.

Warrior gods and gods of the hunt were important deities, most of them being associated with the Sun and the sky. Itzamna, the son of the creator god Hunab Ku, was the head Maya god and Lord of the sky, day and night. The principle Aztec diety was clearly a warrior god. His name, Huitzilopochtli, means "Hummingbird on the Left," or "Reborn Warrior of the South". He was an aspect of the Sun, specifically the Sun at noon, but also was linked to Tezcatlipoca, an older, probably Toltec, warrior god who had four primary manifestations. Since the Aztecs were warriors and empire builders, it stands to reason that these forceful, masculine gods would have become dominant in their religion.

In Aztec mythology, the creator pair Ometecuhtli-Omecihuatl, had four sons. The eldest was the Red Tezcatlipoca, the next the Black Tezcatlipoca. Quetzalcoatl was next, and the Blue Tezcatlipoca last. These four gods were regarded as the primary forces that activate the world, and their battles for supremacy amongst themselves resulted in a series of ages or creations of which we will hear more about later. The colors of the four directions are derived from this quaternary; red given to east, black to north, white to west and blue to south.

Gods of the underworld played a major role in Mesoamerican my-thology. In the Popol Vuh, a surviving work that covers some of the most central myths of the Maya, the heroes of the tale struggle with the Lords of Xibalba, the Maya name for the underworld. Numerous Aztec gods, including Mictlantecuhtli, Xolotl and Tepeyollotl were associated with death, the dark, and the interior of the earth.

Along with the Sun and Moon, the planet Venus was a major deity that had two manifestations associated with its alternating apearance in the east and the west. The man-god Quetzalcoatl, associated with Venus as Morning Star, was a major mythic figure in Mesoamerican high cultures.   He was a teacher and civilizer, but also a man who had sinned. His counter part, the Evening Star, was Xolotl the animal. Of all the celestial bodies, the planet Venus was second in importance only to the Sun, or more accurately, linked to it, and its movements were observed with extreme care.

Space

The Sun, in its demarcation of the directions, is used to define space as well as time. The four directions are determined by the movement of the Sun observed at its rising and setting positions each day. Two times a year, at the equinoxes, the Sun rises exactly east and sets exactly west. At the solstices the Sun reaches its maximum distance from due east or west on the horizon. In summer, the Sun rises and sets to the north of east, in winter to the south of east. For the Mesoamericans, as for all early peoples, this visible solar pattern established a spatial framework that gave structure to the perceived physical world.

As has already been mentioned, the locating and assignment of meaning to the four directions or quarters is the first astrological act. If astrology can be defined as the practical aplication of sky knowledge, that is, the understanding and use of perceived correlations between the heavens and earth, then astrology is not limited to the interpretation of time. The meanings (discovered or assigned) of the four directions establish a grid pattern for future symbolic interpretation. This can be seen in the Western 12-sign zodiac and more directly in the horoscope of 12 houses, which is literally a directional map of the sky.[6] The modern astrology of local space, a branch of astrology that interprets azimuth positions of the planets (at a birth or another specific time) continues the tradition of spatial astrology.

The Mesoamericans recognized a fifth direction, the center, that was also established by the Sun twice a year when it crossed the zenith, the point directly overhead. The zenith transit of the Sun occurs only between the tropics of Cancer and Capricorn which are 23.5 degrees north and south of the Earth's equator. This zone includes Mexico but does not include most of the cultural centers of the Old World. To the Mesoamericans, *the five dimensions of space and the cyclic movement of time were one and the same* since the movements of the Sun defined both. The Sun, as time progressed, was seen to move around the quarters of the world and pass through its center.

The spatial order of the universe, defined by the movements of the Sun on the horizon and at the zenith, was imitated in both the social structure and in the architecture of the Mesoamerican ceremonial center. In both Maya and Aztec cities, the population was usually divided into four districts, each with its own leaders who were ultimately subject to the rule of the principal leader of the city. The great ceremonial centers of Teotihuacan and Tenochtitlan physically consisted of a quartered plaza with large buildings in the center. The pyramid itself, four-sided and peaked in the center, was an embodiment of this pattern. At Teotihuacan the gigantic pyramid of the Sun was constructed so that it directly faced the setting Sun on the day the Sun transited the zenith, a twice yearly occurrence. The major temple of the Aztecs, though reduced now to its lowest levels, is believed to have been oriented in such a way that the equinox Sun rose between the twin temples on its summit when viewed from the temple of Quetzalcoatl facing it.

We have now seen that time and space were one and the same in the Mesoamerican universe and both were established by the Sun. Horizontal space was quartered but vertical space was layered. This is not unlike the Ptolemaic universe in which the various heavens radiated out from the earth at the center. The Mesoamerican conception, however, put an additional series of layers beneath the earth.[7] The scheme probably consisted of the earth as the central layer which counted as number one. Above it were twelve more layers or heavens, and below it eight underworlds. These were expressed as the thirteen heavens (12 +1) and the nine (8 + 1) underworlds, key numbers in the Mesoamerican numerological system. The second layer, immediately above the earth, was associated with the Moon. Above this was the layer of the stars, then that of the Sun and that of Venus. Layer six was the constellation of the fire drill, which was probably located somewhere in the vicinity of the constellation Orion. The seventh layer was that of the green wind, the eighth blue dust and the ninth thunder. The next three layers were the colored zones, white, yellow and red. At the top of

Figure 3. Mesoamerican skywatchers.

the universe was Omeyocan, the realm of the dualistic creator god Ometecuhtli-Omecihuatl, the creator of space, time and the world, and the most remote of the gods.

The layered pattern of the heavens may also have been conceived to be in pyramidal form both above and below the earth. In this view, the thirteen heavens above were arranged such that the seventh heaven was the summit; the first six leading up to it and the second six leading down. The same was true for the nine hells, a descending and ascending succession of 4 levels each with a bottom at the fifth hell. There is a link between this version of the heavens and the pyramid, probably the most sacred architectural form of ancient Mesoamerica. Ceremonies that took place on pyramids were often acts that attempted to recreate the drama of the heavens. The sacrificial victim who climbed the steep steps of a pyramid diagonally was imitating the path of the Sun during the day. At the summit, corresponding to noon and the fifth direction, he was sacrificed, and like the Sun, began his descent.

Time and the 260-Day Calendar

Of even probably even greater importance than sacred space to the ancient peoples of Mesoamerica was the passage of time. Two fundamental calendars were created at some remote time in the past, perhaps during pre-Classic times by the Olmecs. One of these was a civil calendar of 365 days that coincided with the seasons and could be used for agricultural and social purposes. This calendar is often called the "vague year" because it only aproximates the true length of the year which is 365.2422 days. The other was of an odd length, 260 days, that was used for astrological interpretation and prognostication. The Maya word for this calendar was Tzolkin, the Aztec word was Tonalpohualli.[8] The 260-day calendar was composed of 20 named days that repeated 13 times: 13 x 20 = 260. Every 260-day cycle restarted itself regardless of where in the 365-day year it ended. After 52 years of 365 days, and 73 cycles of the 260-day calendar, the two calendars coincided, this period being called the Calendar Round.[9] For the Aztecs, this cycle, called Xuih-molpilli, was a milestone, somewhat like our Western century, and it was celebrated with an elaborate ritual where all fires were extinguished and a new one ignited.

The complex inter-relationships of the 260-day calendar and other time cycles computed by Mesoamerican astronomer/astrologers takes time to fully understand. The material in the next three chapters will be devoted entirely to it.

The Individual, Society and Fate

Interpretive and predictive astrology, defined as the practical aplication of sky and time knowledge, permeated Mesoamerican society. It was concerned with both the affairs of the state and in the lives of individuals. In the ancient centers of Mesoamerica were professionals who specialized in keeping count of the cycles of days for divinatory purposes. Their main tool was the 260-day divinatory calendar, a kind of reference almanac used to determine a person's fate which was said to be indicated by the date on which their birth occurred. It was through the educational system of the priesthood that one could come to a knowledge of the stars and planets. aparently, much study was necessary to master the subject which included both observation and the ability to read the books of pictures and glyphs kept in the temples. Images of Aztec and Maya priests gazing at the sky, sometimes using cross-sticks as if to locate a celestial body with exactness, are found in some of the surviving codices. (See Figure 3.)

Netzahualpilli, the king of Texcoco (one of the Major cities of the Aztec empire), was known for his interest in and knowledge of the stars. He aparently had a roof-top observatory from which he made nightly observations. Post-Conquest sources describe him as eager to speak with anyone in the kingdom who was conversant on the subject. Netzahualpilli was so highly regarded as a skywatcher and prognosticator that he was consulted by the Aztec king Moctezuma (Montezuma) regarding sky omens prior to the arrival of Cortés.

The idea of Fate was deeply rooted in Aztec culture and it was aplied to the entire society itself. For example, the Aztec "Piedra del Sol," or Sun Stone, probably Mexico's most famous symbol, is a complex symbolic depiction of time and the universe with what is believed to be the god Tonatiuh, ruler of the present "sun" or creation, in the center. In the Aztec tradition, this "sun" was the last of 5 "suns" or creations that ruled successive ages. The Aztecs believed that they lived in the fifth or last age which, when its time was up, was to end in destruction by earthquakes. The Maya, who were expert at calculating remote dates, were more specific about such long periods of time, a topic that will be discussed at length in Chapter 7. A Maya creation epoch was a cycle of 13 groups of 144,000 days (each called a baktun) or about 5,125 years. Five of these is 25,627 years which is very close to a precessional cycle of 25,694.8 years.[10] According to Mayan inscriptions, the last age began on August 12, 3114 BC and it will end on December 21, 2012 AD.

The power of astrology and divination on thought and action in ancient Mesoamerica is illustrated by the incredible story of the conquest of the Aztecs by Cortés. At the time, the Aztecs were at the peak of their power and they dominated most of Mesoamerica, with the exception of the Maya regions. Prior to 1519, the year when Cortés arrived, there had been a number of strange events which some of the rulers had interpreted as omens of destruction. In his history, Sahagún describes these omens, one of which is particularly strange.

"Ten years before the Spaniards arrived here, an omen of evil first apeared in the heavens. It was like a tongue of fire, like a flame, like the light of dawn. It looked as if it were showering sparks, as if it stood piercing the heavens. It was wide at the base, it was pointed at the head. For a full year the sign came forth. And when it apeared, there was shouting,.. there was fear...."[11]

Besides this strange light, which some have suggested may have been a comet or an extremely unusual display of the aurora borealis, there was a comet, the accidental burning of the principal temple, and turbulent and destructive waters on the lake which surrounded the city. Moctezuma was aparently so unnerved by the interpretations offered for these omens that he had his astrologers executed. More fortunate, no doubt due to his position, was Nezahualpilli of Texcoco who also warned Moctezuma of possible defeats and disasters.

Aside from these immediate omens was the legend of Quetzalcoatl, a Toltec ruler and the embodiment of Venus who was forced to leave Tula by warrior sorcerers several centuries earlier. He was said to have been born in the year 1-Reed, left in the year 1-Reed, and according to some questionable post-conquest sources, was to return in the year 1-Reed. He had been depicted by the priests as having a beard, wearing a strange helmet and dressed in black! In 1519, which hapened to be the Aztec year 1-Reed, a bearded Cortés landed near present day Veracruz and was contacted by Aztecs.[12] Aztec artists, in the service of Moctezuma, painted Cortés who aparently bore an uncanny resemblance, in attire at least, to certain traditional images of Quetzalcoatl. Spanish gifts, such as a helmet and a deck of cards (4 suits of 13 each totaling 52), also contributed to this association of Cortés with the ancient prophecy. The strange coincidental qualities of this event may have confused the Aztec leader and his will to resist the Spanish invasion seemed to have been seriously damaged. Cortés certainly benefited from this confusion, at least at the outset, and two years later toPled the Aztec empire with only a handful of men.

Among the Maya, a legend of a similar prophecy is found in the Books of Chilam Balam. Chilam Balam (jaguar-priest, a person or a title) is said to have lived at Mani, Yucatan, towards the end of the 15th into the early 16th centuries. To him is credited a prophecy that bearded white men would come from the east during katun 13-Ahau (roughly 1519 to 1539) and establish a new religion. Several versions of this prophecy are found in the various books of Chilam Balam. One of them, found in the Codex Perez and Book of Chilam Balam of Mani, is specific about the day and year that Montejo, the Spanish conqueror of Yucatan, arrived. In this account the prophecy is credited to a priest from the 11th century. As these writings took place well over a hundred years after the conquest, their accuracy is questionable.

In the various versions of the Chilam Balam prophecy is found the notion that the Maya would have to give up the worship of Kukulcan (Quetzalcoatl) when the invaders arrived. More in line with the Aztec legends are some early Spanish translations of a prophecy concerning the return of Quetzalcoatl. aparently they aroused the interest of some of the early missionaries who, by linking Quetzalcoatl with Christ, used them as propaganda for their religion. It has been suggested that the original books of Chilam Balam did contain a prophecy concerning the return of Quetzalcoatl, but in later copies, he was changed to the "bearded white men" and references to Quetzalcoatl were omitted or carefully concealed. Whatever the case, there does apear to have been an original, pre-Conquest prophecy or legend concerning Quetzalcoatl's return throughout ancient Mesoamerica. In both Aztec and Maya cases the prediction was based on recurring cycles of time, a time-period type of astrology which assumes that if a certain combination of cyclic factors correlated with specific events in the past, then similar things would hapen when the patterns repeated themselves. Since the cycles used were based on the astronomical phenomenon, including the diurnal and yearly movements of the Sun, and the cycle of Venus, this is a kind of astrology.

Comparisons With Western Day-Counts

The astrology of ancient Mesoamerica, with the exception of Venus movements, eclipse cycles and planetary stations, was mostly an abstraction of natural cycles. The diurnal movement of the Sun (caused by the rotation of the Earth) was used as a key time unit and meaning was given to various segments of time which were tightly linked to as many natural cycles as possible. This deification of time, or time-period astrology, is similar in principle to one that evolved in the ancient Near East and which survives in a form in Western culture today -- the planetary week and its hours. A digression on this subject will perhaps put the Mesoamerican system in better perspective.

The seven days of the week we use in our civil calendar are named for the seven visible planets. The order of the planetary week (Sunday, Monday, Tuesday, etc. gives us this sequence of planets: Sun, Moon, Mars, Mercury, Jupiter, Venus and Saturn. The Nordic names used in English are apropriate substitutes for the planetary names which are aparent in the Romance languages. This order does not apear to make any astronomical sense until we recognize that it is a secondary sequence based on a primary order of the hours of the day, called the Chaldean order. This sequence, based on the increasing average daily motions of the seven visible planets, is Saturn, Jupiter, Mars, Sun, Venus, Mercury and Moon. Saturn has the least average movement per day while the Moon has the most. Each day and each night is divided into twelve equal hours, with the lengths varying, depending on the season. Each hour is ruled by a planet and the sequence of planetary hours is the Chaldean order. The planet that rules the first hour of the day gives its name to that day. Since there are 24 hours in a full day and there are 7 planets, each succeeding day is ruled by the third planet ahead in the Chaldean order from the ruler of the previous day. For example, we could start with Saturday which is ruled by Saturn. Saturn rules the 1st, 8th, 15th and 22nd hours of that day. Then Jupiter will rule the 23rd, and Mars the 24th and last hour. The Sun will then rule the first hour of the next day and it will give its name to Sunday.

The origins of the Western 7-day planetary week are not exactly clear. Traditionally, the Greeks used months of 30 days divided into three 10-day weeks, and the Romans used an 8-day week. It apears that the 7-day week, or septimana, was brought to Greece and Rome from Alexandria, that melting-pot of Near Eastern knowledge.[13] This probably occurred during the Hellenistic period, the time between the flowering of Greece and the Roman Empire. Later, the Romans spread it throughout their empire. The Roman historian Dion Cassius attributes it to the Jews who worshiped on Saturn's day, but it is unlikely that a monotheistic group would create a week named after several gods.[14] Most probably, the 7-day planetary week had its origins in the merging of Mesopotamian, Egyptian and Greek time reckoning systems following Alexander's empire in the 3rd century BC.

During the Roman empire the 7-day week was probably used to some extent as a kind of divinatory guide. The Roman historian Suetonius notes that the emperor Tiberius thought Saturday a bad day to begin a journey. Later, the Romans made Sunday the first day of the week and it came to be associated with Christianity. It seems that the origins of this custom may have had roots in the popular religions of Sun worship and Mithraism.

In the tradition of the planetary week, births occur on a day ruled by a particular planet, and also during an hour. This information could be used to make a determination as to what an individual's fate might be. An old, yet still familiar, children's poem has preserved this tradition.

"Monday's child is fair in face;
Tuesday's child is full of grace;
Wednesday's child is full of woe;
Thursday's child has far to go;
Friday's child is loving and giving;
Saturday's child works hard for its living.
But the child that is born on the Sabbath day
is bonnie and bright and good and day. "[15]

This kind of "day" astrology was known in the ancient Western world and also during the Middle Ages when predictions for the year itself were based on the day of the week on which Christmas or the first day of the year fell. Here is an astrology of time, number and rulership. The basic unit of the day, created by the Sun, is divided into sections of time that are given meanings, as is the day itself. As we will see, the Mesoamericans were not so different from us in this respect, they just developed a different numerology and took the idea a little further.

Chapter 3

The 260-Day Astrological Calendar

One of the most original astro-numerological divinatory systems ever produced by any culture was a 260-day count or calendar called the Tonalpohualli by the Aztecs, the Tzolkin by the Maya and the Piye by the Zapotecs. Surviving intact (more or less) into modern times, this time-count consists of a sequence of 20 named days (day-signs) and 13 numbers that cycle until all 260 possible combinations occur. The count is continuous; the cycle starts again as soon as 260 days have passed. In ancient times this calendar ran alongside the civil or vague year of 365 days (not to be confused with the Maya tun of 360 days), with the two cycles meshing at the same point every 52 years. The meeting of the two calendars, after 73 cycles of 260 days and 52 years, is called the calendar round or the Mesoamerican century. The Aztecs called it the Xuihmolpilli, the Maya name is unknown.

The origins of the 260-day period are unclear. The earliest glyphs of day-signs, found near Monte Alban, date to about -600. Why there are 260 days is debatable. It has been suggested that this interval was derived from the zenith passage of the Sun at the latitude of Copan and Izapa, two early cultural centers located at 15 degrees north latitude.[1] At these sites, the Sun spends 105 days north of the zenith and 260 days south of it. Further, one of the two dates of the Sun's zenith passage turns out to be August 12, the zero date of the Maya Long Count, a 5,125 year period discussed in Chapter 7. There is much evidence throughout Mesoamerica that zenith passages (the fifth direction) were considered to be extremely important and were used to date important rituals and other activities.[2]

Another explanation is that 260 days is about equal to the human gestation period. Nine months (moons) of just under 29 days is close to this figure. In fact, this is the answer given today by Maya daykeepers who continue to use the count as a ritual almanac and system of divination. Since the 260-day count is subdivided into 20 periods of 13 numbered days each, it may be that the daily motion of the Moon had some bearing on the creation of this period. The average distance in longitude that the Moon travels in one day is roughly 13 degrees. In traditional Western astrology, this distance is known as a lunar mansion. The Sun travels about one degree per day and would therefore cover this distance in 13 days. Since it has also been suggested that the number 20 derives from the number of digits on the human body, 10 fingers and 10 toes, the 260-day count may be a blend of "facts" taken from both human anatomy and the heavens.

Archaeoastronomers who study Mesoamerican astronomy and calendrics have forwarded other purely astronomical reasons to explain the 260-day count. Eclipses occur when the Sun and Moon are near the Moon's nodes, an interval of 173.31 days. This period, called an eclipse half-year, is proportional to the 260 day count in the ratio of 3:2. Three eclipse half years equals 519.93 days, very close to 2 x 260 or 520. Further, the synodic period of Mars, that is the interval between successive conjunctions or other aspects to the Sun, equals 780 days or 3 x 260. The appearance intervals of Venus, its periods as a morning or evening star, are about 263 days on average, closely approximating the 260-day tonalpohualli/tzolkin. A very complex, but compelling, argument was made by Seler, a pioneer in the field. He suggested that the figure 260 is a natural result of a numerological exercise involving figures for the solar year and the Venus synodical year. His logic is explained in chapter six. Perhaps the 260-day count is something like a hard-working lowest common denominator, an interval which has links to many other important astronomically determined intervals. [3]

The twenty day-signs or named days, like our Western 7-day week, repeat in their order continuously. More than just names, they are a sequence of archetypal symbols of the Mesoamerican universe. They are in some ways similar to the 22 cards of the major arcana in the Tarot, each card being symbolic of a key theme in human life. They are also similar to the signs of the Greek/Babylonian zodiac, but they symbolize the differing qualities of *blocks of time,* not sections

1 2 3 4

5 6 7 8

9 10 11 12

13 14 15 16

17 18 19 20

Figure 4. The Aztec symbols of the twenty day-signs.

Figure 5. The Maya symbols of the twenty day-signs.

of space in the sky. Each of the twenty day-signs, called tonalli by the Aztecs (the Maya word is unknown), is linked with one of the primary gods of their pantheon who has rulership over that day and therefore influences its meaning. Less is known about the linkage between the twenty days and Maya deities. The names of the individual day-signs often have several meanings that play a major role in elucidating the symbol. There are stylized glyphs for each day, both Aztec and Maya, illustrated in Figures 4 and 5. The entire sequence of the 260-day count of twenty days and thirteen numbers is found in several of the ancient books that survived the great book burnings shortly following the Spanish conquest of Mexico. Called by the Aztecs Tonalamatl, which means "book of fate" or "book of the days", these books of symbolic pictures were used by both priests and divination experts as a source book of interpretation, much like the I-Ching of the Chinese.

The 20 day-signs, with simple English translations, are listed below in their universal sequence. While there are some variants between the Aztec, Yucatec Maya and Quiche Maya versions, the consistency among them is apparent. A more complete description of the internal logic of this sequence is found in the next chapter.

Aztec/Nahuatl	Yucatec Maya
1. Cipactli (crocodile, alligator)	Imix (sea dragon, water)
2. Ehecatl (wind)	Ik (air, life)
3. Calli (house)	Akbal (night)
4. Cuetzpallin (lizard)	Kan (corn)
5. Coatl (serpent)	Chicchan (serpent)
6. Miquiztli (death)	Cimi (death)
7. Mazatl (deer)	Manik (deer, grasp)
8. Tochtli (rabbit)	Lamat (rabbit)
9. Atl (water)	Muluc (water/rain)
10. Itzcuintli (dog)	Oc (dog)
11. Ozomatli (monkey)	Chuen (monkey)
12. Malinalli (grass)	Eb (broom)
13. Acatl (reed)	Ben (reed)
14. Ocelotl (ocelot)	Ix (jaguar, magician)

15. Cuauhtli (eagle)   Men (eagle, wise one)
16. Cozcacuauhtli (vulture)   Cib (owl, vulture)
17. Ollin (motion-earthquake)   Caban (force, earth)
18. Tecpatl (flint knife)   Etz'nab (flint knife)
19. Quiahuitl (rain)   Cauac (storm)
20. Xochitl (flower)   Ahau (Lord)

Quiche Maya

1. Imox (crocodile)   11. Batz' (monkey)
2. Ik' (wind)   12. E (tooth)
3. Ak'abal (night)   13. Aj (cane)
4. C'at (lizard)   14. Ix (jaguar)
5. Can (serpent)1   5. Tz'iquin (bird)
6. Came (death)   16. Ajmac (owl)
7. Quej (deer)   17. No'j (incense)
8. K'anil (rabbit)   18. Tijax (flint)
9. Toj (storm)   19. Cawuk (storm)
10. Tz'i' (dog)   20. Junajpu (hunter)

One can see that the Aztec and Maya versions of the 20 day-signs are basically similar. This is true also for the Zapotec version and those of other culturally related groups in the Mesoamerican region. What is common to all versions of this twenty-day sequence, is the notion that a birth occurring on any particular day will be influenced by the symbolic nature of that day. In ancient times, newborn babies were taken to an astrologer, calendar expert or priest who could read the Tonalamatl or book of fate. Such an astrologer was known to the Aztecs as a tonalpouhque. In his book on the calendar, Fray Diego Durán wrote;

"Thus, when a boy or girl was born, the father or relatives of the babe immediately went to visit the astrologers, sorcerers, or soothsayers, who were plentiful, begging them to state the destiny of the newborn boy or girl. The inquirer always carried with him offerings of food and drink. The astrologer and sorcerer- fortune-teller brought out the Book of the Horoscope, together with the calendar. Once the character of the day had

been seen, prophecies were uttered, lots were cast, and a propitious or evil fate for the babe was determined by the consultation of a paper painted with all the gods they adored, each idol drawn in the square reserved for him. "[4]

While the fates of the 260-day count were very specific and rigid, efforts to alter the fate of a newborn were often made. Among the Aztecs, at least, it was apparently common to delay the announcement of a birth for a few days until a more favorable day had arrived. Besides the child's fate, a personal name was sometimes determined by the combination of day name and number. For example, one could have the name 8-Rabbit, or perhaps 2- Serpent, followed by another given name. In this astrology of ancient Mesoamerica, the temperament, disposition and even future occupation were believed to be determined by the symbolic charac-teristics of the birthday.

The 260-day count was also used as a means of electing a day to commence particular activities. For example, it was said that merchants would wait until the day 1-Serpent to begin long journeys to buy and sell merchandise. Other dates favorable for starting ventures were related to 1-Serpent within the context of the 260-day calendar. For example, the day 1-Monkey, which stands 26 days or two 13-day units ahead of 1-Serpent, was also considered auspicious. Even war was timed by the occurrence of this particular day. Fray Bernardino De Sahagun wrote;

"Likewise it was said that at the time of the day sign One Serpent, if it was established precisely at that time, when war was declared and proclaimed among the people, when, it was said, war was announced, at that very time war began. At that time all the eagle and ocelot warriors set out to battle; all followed, crowded, and filled the road.   They arose, they set out, departed, marched, and hastened." [5]

Among the present day Quiche Maya of Guatamala, the 260-day count is used similarly, as a means of reckoning the quality of a given day and also as a mental divination board. Like the Tarot or the I Ching, the sequence of numbers and names make up a complex arrangement of symbols. Practitioners called day-keepers randomly grab seeds and crystals out of a bag, which when counted out, direct the inquirer to a specific number and sign. The proper interpretation of this number and sign, along with knowledge of the inquirers' birth date, provides the basis for the reader to meet the needs of his client. Thus in Guatamala the day-keeper is both a calendar expert and a divination consultant. This may have also been true in ancient times. [6]

Aztec, Classic and modern Maya versions of this 20-day sequence all follow the same pattern in terms of numbering. As was mentioned earlier, each day was numbered from one to thirteen, this generating 260 possible combinations. Imagine two gears, one with 13 teeth and the other with 20, both turning against each other. Only after 20 revolutions of the 13-tooth gear and 13 of the 20- tooth do the same teeth meet. To illustrate further, suppose we start with 1-Alligator. Next would come 2-Wind, then 3-House, etc. After 13-Reed, the count would begin again at 1-Ocelot, then 2-Eagle, 3-Vulture, etc. (For further clarification, study Table 2 in Chapter 9.) The number associated with each day was central in determining the quality of any particular day. To the Aztecs, 3 of any named day was generally lucky or favorable, 4 and 7 were neutral, 9 was harmful and the last four were favorable with some reservations. The Quiche Maya consider the early numbers to represent something youthful or developing, while the later numbers suggest old, or completed development.

When a day is prefixed by the number one, it becomes a dominant influence for the full period of the next thirteen days. In a sense, it becomes ruler of a 13-day week, or as Sahagun calls it, a sign. This period is also often referred to as the trecena, Spanish for "the thirteen." Each trecena had its own set of symbols and a ruling deity that was different from the symbolism of the named day from which the name of the period was derived.   A person's birthday was then designated by both trecena and day sign and it appears that each trecena had a modifying effect on any births that took place during its rule. For example, a birthday might be given as occurring during the trecena 1-Reed and on the day 5-Earthquake. Further, there would be a month and day of the civil solar calendar to further define the uniqueness of the day. Following is a list of the 13-day periods, the second sequence of the twenty named days, and the one often found in the surviving manuscripts. English translation of the Aztec names are used. The next chapter contains further information about this sequence including the associated symbols and gods.

The sequence of the twenty 13-day periods or trecena

1. 1-Crocodile	11. 1-Monkey
2. 1-Ocelot	12. 1-Lizard
3. 1-Deer	13. 1-Earthquake
4. 1-Flower	14. 1-Dog
5. 1-Reed	15. 1-House
6. 1-Death	16. 1-Vulture
7. 1-Rain	17. 1-Water
8. 1-Grass	18. 1-Wind
9. 1-Serpent	19. 1-Eagle
10. 1-Knife	20. 1-Rabbit

The Calendar, the Names of the Years, and the Four Directions

Of the 20 day-signs, only four could fall on the first day of any given 365-day year.[7] The civil, or agricultural, year of 365 days was divided into 18 months of 20 days each with 5 extra days. The Maya called this calendar the Haab. Assuming we were to start the count of the 20 day-signs or tonalli on the first day of the year, we would see 18 repetitions of the cycle plus five more days and would end up 5 days ahead in the count. The year following would then begin 5 days ahead of this particular day-sign. Since there are only 20 tonalli, after four years had passed, the year would once again begin with the same day we originally started with. During Aztec times these four days, called the year bearers, were Acatl (Reed), Tecpatl (Knife), Calli (House) and Tochtli (Rabbit). During classic Maya times the year bearers were Ix (Jaguar), Manik (Deer), Eb (Broom) and Caban (Earthquake). At the time of the Spanish Conquest however, Landa reported that the Maya rulers of the year were Kan (Corn), Muluc (Water), Ix (Wind) and Cauac (Rain). While the same calendrical pattern was applied throughout Mesoamerica, the actual timing was not consistent. Surviving documents indicate that during Post Classic

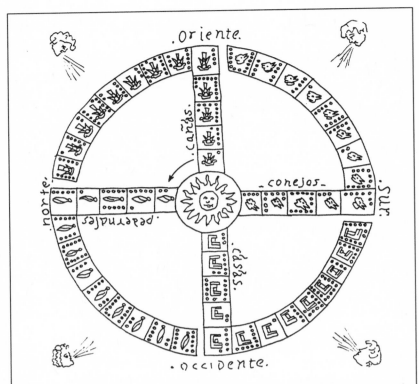

Figure 6. A diagram from Duran showing the order of the signs in the 52-year cycle of the yearbearers. The cycle begins with the sign 1-Reed and moves counter-clockwise to 2-Knife, 3-House, 4- Rabbit, 5-Reed, etc.

times the year bearers were moved ahead twice, the last adjustment being the one recorded by Landa. Why this was done is still a mystery. Interestingly, the modern day Quiche Maya use the same year bearers as did the classic Maya.

The year bearers designated the ruling deities of any particular year, gave it a specific name, and were also used to forecast the nature of the year. Since each of the day-signs were also numbered, as we will see below, each year bearer would have a number from one to thirteen. For example, if the day sign 1-Reed occurred on the first day of the year, 2-Knife would occur exactly one year later. The year after that would begin with 3-House and the year after that with 4-Rabbit. 5-Reed would begin the fifth year. After each year bearer occurred thirteen times, the calendar round was completed: 4 x 13 = 52 years.

In the diagram from Durán below (Figure 6.) the sequence of the years and their relationship to the four directions is shown. East is at the top, north to the left, etc. Beginning with 1- Reed, immediately above the Sun in the center of the diagram, the cycle of the years moves counter-clockwise and out from spoke to spoke until 4-Reed, at the top of the Reed or eastern spoke is reached. From here, the years are shown as part of the outside circle, but in the same counter-clockwise and forward-moving sequence ending with 13-Rabbit.

Durán reported that years beginning with the day Reed, associated with the east, were said to be good, fertile and abundant years. The years beginning with Knife and House, linked to the west and north, were considered unfavorable. Knife was barren, fruitless and dry while House brought clouds, mist and rain. The years beginning with the day Rabbit, the sign of the south, were of a mixed quality, some being good while others bad.[8]

Landa likewise wrote of the fortunes and the necessary rituals the Maya associated with the four rulers of the years. In the Maya calendar of Landa's time, which was basically the same as that of the Aztecs, the four days that occurred at the beginning of the year were Kan, Muluc, Ix and Cauac. Their Aztec correspondences would be Lizard, Water, Ocelot, and Rain. In Maya mythology and cosmology, these four days, called the bacabs, were the four supporters of the world who were positioned at the four quarters. The east was linked with Muluc and was considered a favorable year, the best of the four. Ix, the bacab of the north, was said to be a bad year, ill-omened and filled with shortages of water, hot spells and hunger. Men who sought to be chiefs would fail and there would be changes in rulership due to discord and war. Cauac, the western bacab, was also held to be bad, particularly for agriculture. Kan, the ruler of the south, was basically good, but elaborate ceremonies (also done in the other years) were necessary to insure this.[9]

Although the actual named days which fell on the first of the year in the Aztec and Maya calendars were different, the divinatory meanings of the four directions was similar. Both Reed and Muluc, associated with the east, were said to be favorable years while Ix and

Knife, linked to the north, were bad years. House/Cauac and Rabbit/Kan also had similar divinatory meanings when they began a year. There is a consistency in the association of directions. The sequence of the twenty days usually begins with the day-sign Crocodile or Alligator, which is a sign of emergence and creation. This sign is traditionally assigned to the east, beginning the sequence east, north, west, south. In this scheme both Reed and Muluc emerge as signs of the east. The other Aztec and Maya year-bearers match up direction-wise also. The list below illustrates this pattern within the basic sequence of the day-signs.

Figure 7a. The Codex Fejervary-Mayer cosmogram.

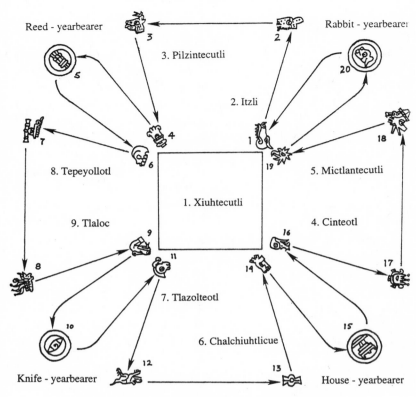

Figure 7b. The layout of the Fejervary-Mayer cosmogram.

Aztec/Maya

East	Cipactli/Imix - crocodile
North	Ehecatl/Ik - wind
West	Calli/Akbal - house/night
South	Cuetzpallin/Kan - lizard/corn
East	Coatl/Chiccan - serpent
North	Miquiztli/Cimi - death/skull
West	Mazatl/Manik - deer/grasp
South	Tochtli/Lamat - rabbit
East	Atl/Muluc - water
North	Itzcuintli/Oc - dog
West	Ozomatli/Chuen - monkey
South	Malinalli/Eb - grass/broom

East	Acatl/Ben - reed
North	Ocelotl/Ix - jaguar
West	Cuauhtli/Men - eagle
South	Cozcacuauhtli/Cib - vulture/owl
East	Ollin/Caban - movement/earthquake
North	Tecpatl/Etz'nab - flint/knife
West	Quiahuitl/Cauac - rain/storm
South	Xochitl/Ahau - flower/lord

Many diagrams showing various arrangements of the day-signs have survived. They are essentially efforts to picture the universe as the ancient Mesoamericans saw it - a center with four directions supporting the material universe, with the day-signs as focused expressions of the creative force behind everything. An excellent example of such a diagram is the Mixtec calendar from the Codex Fejervary-Mayer, Figure 7.

The border of this cosmogram is marked with 260 small circles at intervals of thirteen, marked by each of the twenty signs. This progression begins in the upper right hand corner and moves counter clockwise. The four arms of the cross and the center symbolize the five regions or divisions of the world. East is at the top, south to the right, west at the bottom and north on the left. The Sun is located in the east just above the center. The year bearers, Reed/East, Rabbit/South, House/West and Knife/North, prominently occupy the four corners of the design. In the center is Xiuhtecuhtli, the lord of central fire, being fed blood (jagged lines) from the rest of the diagram. He is surrounded by 8 other deities who appear in the four directions around him. These nine gods are the Lords of the Night which will be discussed later.

In this and other cosmic pictograms from the Maya and Aztec cultures, ancient artists have tried to show the order and inter-connectedness of the universe as it was perceived in pre- Columbian times. The rhythm of the days, time, the four primary directions, and space, are captured in paint in two dimensions. Like a Buddhist mandala these cosmograms are both centering and enlightening, allowing one to enter into an understanding of the central workings of their universe, and perhaps our own to some extent. Astrology, the symbolism of the sky acting on the earth and giving form to reality, is shown in these cosmograms as the succession of named days. The day-signs encircle the center and the creation of the world itself, and are steadied by the four directions.

Chapter 4

The Twenty Named Days

The twenty day-signs of the 260-day count repeat endlessly like those of our Western seven-day planetary week. As pictured in the codices, each day in the Aztec version of this cycle had a glyph or symbolic picture and was associated with a deity from the Aztec pantheon. In most cases, it is this deity that best expresses the meaning of the sign. The Maya version also had glyphs, though far more abstract and stylized, and fewer correlations between days and deities are known. A listing of the day- signs and their Aztec god rulerships appears below.

Day-Sign/Aztec God

1. Alligator - Tonacatecuhtli
2. Wind - Ehecatl
3. House - Tepeyollotl
4. Lizard - Ueuecoyotl
5. Serpent - Chalchihuitlicue
6. Death - Tecciztecatl
7. Deer - Tlaloc
8. Rabbit - Mayauel
9. Water - Xiuhtecuhtli
10. Dog - Mictlantecuhtli
11. Monkey - Xochipilli
12. Grass - Patecatl
13. Reed - Tezcatlipoca
14. Ocelot - Tlazolteotl
15. Eagle - Xipe Totec
16. Vulture - Itzpapalotl
17. Earthquake - Xolotl
18. Knife - Chalchiuhtotolin
19. Rain - Tonatiuh
20. Flower - Xochiquetzal

In this chapter we will attempt to understand what is known about each of the twenty days used by the Aztecs and Maya. Where appropriate, and to clarify ambiguities, Zapotec and Quiche Maya versions of the 20-day sequence will be referred to. Sources of information include the writings of Eduard Seler, a pioneering interpreter of

Mesoamerican codices at the beginning of this century, and J. Eric S. Thompson, whose landmark book Maya Hieroglyphic Writing has contributed much useful information about the day-signs. Both authors are academic in their approach; their efforts to grasp the nature of the day-signs suffer from their lack of experience in working with a symbolic language. However, they are thorough in accumulating data, and their material is invaluable for the task of sorting through what are only traces of the ancient astrological system. In contrast to the academic tradition, several indigenous publications have contributed useful insights. In today's Mexico, Aztec descendants are striving to recapture their heritage. In pre-Conquest times, the population of Mexico-Tenochtitlan was divided into about twenty territorial units called calpulli, each of which had a special interest or function. Several of these survive; one that calls itself Kalpulli Toltekayotl has published an Aztec calendar that tracks the day-signs and contains some ideas about the gods that rule the signs. In the day-sign text that follows, I refer in places to the author of this calendar, Arturo Meza Gutierrez.

Post-conquest sources, including the writings of Sahagún and Durán, were compiled after the Mexican holocaust of conquest and disease occurred, which eliminated most of the population and presumably, most of the learned astrologers and priests. Durán's writings on the day-signs are scant while Sahagún's longer reports are distorted and were probably given to him by amateurs. Nonetheless, they are among the few scraps we have that describe the day-signs as they were used and understood in the 16th century. One of these scraps (see Figure 8) is a drawing that shows correlations between the day-signs and the parts of the human body.

Besides the above mentioned sources, I have tried using common sense, something often forgotten by more academic researchers. For example, the use of a particular animal to symbolize a day- sign is probably very important. Animals, a major part of daily life in ancient times, have specific characteristics that embody or describe the principles that the day-sign represents. In the Western zodiac animals are used to illustrate the nature of the signs -- why should not that be also the case here? Meanings can also be deduced linguistically. Each sign has many names, in Aztec, Maya, Zapotec,

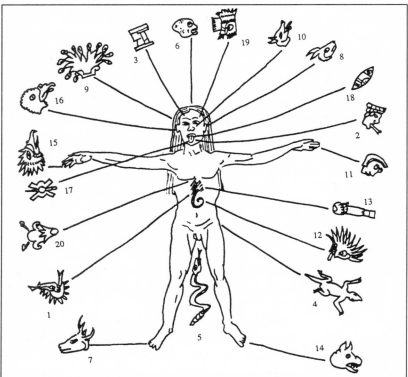

Figure 8. The correspondences of the day-signs with the human body from Codex Vaticanus A.

and many other Mesoamerican dialects, and each name has a translation which may differ from that of another region. Frequently the names, while different, do point to a common theme and therefore a common interpretation. For the reader's convenience, English translations of Aztec (Nahuatl) and Classic Maya names for the day-signs will be used to introduce the sign and that name will be used frequently throughout the rest of the book. As you read the following discussions, be aware that my purpose is to present a good sampling of what the main sources have to say about the day-signs, not to frustrate the reader. As you will soon realize, understanding the day-signs is not easy. How easy would it be to offer delineations of the signs of the Western zodiac if all that was known about them were their names, their symbols, and maybe one or two keywords? I want readers to understand how much knowledge has been lost by being exposed to the often contradictory information that the main sources offer. Readers should also keep in mind that the negative tone of many of the delineations may be due in part to the lack of reliable sources, but more likely it is simply a reflection of how the world was experienced. Negative astrological delineations are also found in astrological texts from the ancient Greco-Roman world. The working delineations of the day-signs presented later in this book (and also in my book Day-Signs) are founded on these down-to-eath sources, though they have been developed and greatly elaborated upon.

Crocodile/Cipactli/Imix

The day-sign known as crocodile or alligator is commonly considered the first of the days (at least in ancient times). The Aztec name for this day is Cipactli, which means something like "prickly object". The word itself may have referred to a plant with an edible root or perhaps to the alligator or crocodile. The Zapotec word clearly refers to alligator or crocodile which, in myth, floated on a great pond and whose back was the Earth itself. The Aztec symbol for this day was the head of an alligator or crocodile with a row of spines along its back, but without a lower jaw. In Aztec creation mythology, the great god Tezcatlipoca ripped off the jaw of this earth monster when he pulled her out of the primeval depths. In essence, the symbol suggests the creation of the world that we inhabit. Supporting this notion is the fact that the Aztec deity, Ometecuhtli/Tonacatecuhtli, the dualistic creator god, was associated with the day-sign. Ometecuhtli/Tonacatecuhtli is actually the male component of a duality who were the principal generators and creators of all existence. Along with his female counterpart, Omecihuatl/Tonacacihuatl, this god-pair lives in the highest of thirteen heavens.

The Maya name, Imix or Imox, is a word that seems to refer to the earth god and consequently, the Earth itself. The Mayan glyph for the day has been compared to a woman's nipple, a symbol of nourishment. Thompson thinks it to be a depiction of the water lily, also a symbol of nourishment and one connected to aquatic reptiles.

Among various Maya tribes, this day-sign is linked with the earth and its bounty, including food. In the Maya account of the creation (Chumayel), four trees are located at the four directions or corners of the world. The trees are called Imix ayaxche. Thompson notes that in one Yucatec village the fruits of the yaxche or ch'oy trees are to be avoided by young girls as they cause the breasts to grow large, which suggests a link with the creation trees and nourishment. There are also connections with the ceiba tree, a giant tree usually found growing in the old town plazas that symbolizes growth from deep within the earth (from it's core to be exact).

Given the above information, one would assume that this day-sign was a symbol for the creation, for Mother Earth, and for the abundance and nourishment which the Earth provides. The crocodile or alligator as a symbol makes good sense when one considers the function and habits of that creature, something the indigenous peoples undoubtedly did. Alligators and crocodiles are reptiles with an unusually strong maternal instinct. Some species lay their eggs and wait by them until they hatch, then lead their young into the water. Unlike snakes or turtles, young alligators will remain near their mother for some time, climbing on her back for sun and protection. Alligators also create living space for other creatures when they make nests in swampy waters. Their circular clearings keep the water deep enough for certain species of fish and other aquatic life to prosper. Through its nesting efforts, the alligator is actually a very important aspect of the life chain in areas such as Florida's Everglades, and one would assume, in the similar swampy wetlands and inlets in the Yucatan. In Mexico, crocodiles are found along the east coast, alligators along the west. In this book I refer to this sign as both Alligator and Crocodile.

Wind/Ehecatl/Ik

The Aztec name for this day-sign is Ehecatl, the wind-god. Ehecatl was a manifestation of the god or man-god Quetzalcoatl. The day-sign was depicted by the long, red-snouted mask worn by Quetzalcoatl, through which the wind (the breath of Ehecatl) blew. Wind and breath are linked here and funneled through the snout of a major deity, a deity of knowledge. For the Aztecs, Wind was the breath of life and the movement of intelligence through the human mind.

Although the Zapotec name for this day was "fire," the Maya name Ik also meant wind, breath and life, suggesting a concept like "the breath of life."The glyph for this day-sign, which usually included a "T" design, had associations with a god of rains as well as wind.[1] Rains are needed to germinate seeds and stimulate life, and this "coming to life" may be the meaning the Maya intended.

Given the above information, it would appear that the day-sign Wind was a symbol for life and possibly intelligence. The Aztec association with Quetzalcoatl is interesting as this god represents the intelligence of Man, as well as his flaws. Durán writes that a feast to the air and Ehecatl were celebrated during pre-Conquest times in Cholula, an old and important city in central Mexico.[2] He reports connections between this city and Quetzalcoatl who was a god of merchants, a master of marketing, and cutter of gemstones. All of this suggests that wind, air, Cholula and Quetzalcoatl represent cleverness and skill, perhaps even intelligence.

When one considers what wind is like, a few more ideas are generated. Wind is felt, but not seen directly, and it can often make itself known unpredictably. Wind animates things -- it seems to make trees and rocks talk. Durán mentions in his brief section on Ehecatl and the feast of Air that the Aztecs were fearful of the "talking of the wind."

House/Calli/Akbal

The day-sign Calli, translated from the Aztec language nahuatl, means "house." The symbol used for that day was a sectioned temple, often showing a staircase. The god Tepeyollotl, whose name means "heart of the mountains," was its ruling deity. Tepeyollotl, one of the nine Lords of the Night, was a jaguar god, an aspect of the Sun when under the Earth at night, and also the cause of earthquakes, volcanoes, and eruptions. He was a god of interiors, caves, darkness and the night. One interesting association with Tepeyollotl is that of echoes. Echoes are produced by sound bouncing around in caves and enclosed structures. The Zapotec name for this sign, Ela, means night.

Akbal is the Maya name for this day-sign and it, too, means darkness or night. Another Maya name is Uotan, meaning "heart," which had associations with Earth gods and the drum. According to Thompson, the glyph for Akbal may signify an animal of the underworld, perhaps the jaguar. All told, the Maya description of this day-sign does not seem very different from that of the Aztecs.

Clearly, House is a sign of both darkness and interiors. It suggests forces at work that are not seen in the light of day, yet forces, such as earthquakes, that are quite powerful. There is an association with the jaguar, a nocturnal animal, suggesting unseen, uncontrollable, and potentially dangerous forces. The use of a temple as a symbol is interesting. Anyone who has entered an ancient Mexican temple knows how dark such windowless structures can be. Gutierrez connects this sign with the idea of internal knowledge and the secrets of the subconscious. It may be dark inside a cave or a temple, but, more importantly, in this darkness ordinary reality ceases to exist and other kinds of consciousness can rise from the depths of the mind. Echoes, which one hears inside a temple, and drums are both suggestive of sound in closed spaces.

Lizard/Cuetzpallin/Kan

While the Aztec word for this day-sign, Cuetzpallin, means "lizard," the Maya name Kan means "ripe corn." To further complicate matters, the Zapotec name can be translated as either "frog," "toad," or "roasted corn." Obviously an understanding of the nature of this day requires a reconciliation between these different symbols.

In the Aztec and Mixtec manuscripts, the sign is depicted as a long-tailed lizard often colored blue. The animal referred to could possibly be the common Mexican iguana. The day-sign was associated with an ancient god called Ueuecoyotl, a crafty coyote god of the dance known for his sexual activities. Gutierrez connects this god with ceremonial dance and the energy (basically sexual energy) generated by such an activity.

The Maya called this day Kan, which suggests corn and ripeness.

The highly stylized glyph for the day does not offer much of a clue, though young maize plants are shown growing from the Kan glyph in the codices. The Kan glyph, often painted yellow, is also found in the codices near offerings of food, which suggests that corn, the most important food of the Maya, was simply a reference to that which sustains life.

A common link between the Aztec and Maya versions of this sign is not obvious. But perhaps a beginning can be made by looking from a common-sense point of view. The lizard, probably the iguana, is a large and edible animal. Lizards normally remain motionless for long periods of time but are capable of very swift and unpredictable movements. They live by themselves, the females abandoning her eggs and letting the baby lizards fend for themselves. For a time the lizards herd together, but soon they go their separate ways. Could the sign signify unpredictable behavior, does it depict the solitary condition of full adulthood (ripening), or does it signify food?

When one considers ripe corn as a symbol for the day-sign, the idea that comes to mind is completion, maturity, or full growth. The ripe ear of corn is not only ready for consumption, it has completed its life cycle and is capable of reproducing the plant from which it came. Ripe corn is the seed of the plant, it contains within itself the potential of renewed life. Probably for both reasons, edible food and potential future food, the ripe ear of corn would have been highly valued.

Perhaps the reconciliation here lies in the notion of completion and potential for creation. The lizard, a solitary animal, does not need a community, it lives out its life as an individual. The ear of corn is the completion of the corn plant, it needs no more growth. The Zapotec frog or toad symbolism also suggests the idea of completion, from egg to tadpole to adult amphibian. The association of the god Ueuecoyotl with the day-sign Lizard suggests that sexuality, a mysterious force which sustains life, was also a theme of this sign; correspondingly the ear of corn is the part of the plant that can reproduce itself. Finally, both items, lizard and corn, can be eaten and are nourishing. Though the matter is far from resolved, perhaps one could say that the day-sign Lizard symbolizes sexual maturity and the capacity to reproduce. This attainment is an act of individuality, a separation from dependence on the group or the parent plant.

Serpent/Coatl/Chicchan

The Aztec name for this sign, Coatl, and the Maya name Chicchan, both mean snake or serpent. In the Aztec tradition, this day-sign was depicted by a the head of a snake, one of the symbols of Chalchihuitlicue, the beautiful young goddess of ground water and springs. She also represented both the temporary beauty of nature and its destructive power, in the form of storms and whirlpools. Chalchihuitlicue and the serpent were probably symbols of the latent, though powerful, transforming energies of nature itself.

To the Maya, this sign suggested the celestial serpents, located at the four quarters, that were linked to rainfall. The glyph itself suggests the head or scales of a snake, and in the codices it is linked to a serpent god. The Zapotec word for this day does not imply serpent, but something like "sinister omen."

Over 450 species of snakes can be found in Mexico; they are animals that evoke fear and awe, and are frequently accorded sexual power. The snake is an animal that has a primitive form, simply a spine with a head. It sheds its skin regularly in order to grow and it lives within the earth. This ability to transform itself, to discard the past, and also its secret life in the dark interior of the earth, suggest that it was a symbol of mysterious, and at times threatening, forces. The link with rain storms may have to do with the behavior of certain species of snakes during or prior to rains. The association with Chalchiuhtilicue, and therefore springs and ground water, may have something to do with the secret life of snakes below the ground.

Serpent appears to be a symbol of the source of the powerful transforming forces of nature that are basically mysterious. It probably also symbolizes the renewal of life itself, as shown by both the shedding of skin and the water "born" from the earth at a spring.

Death/Miquiztli/Cimi

Miquiztli is the Aztec name for this sign and its symbol was the skull. The Aztec deity was Tecciztecatl, the male form of the Moon, depicted as an old man carrying a seashell on his back. In the story of the creation of the present age, recounted by Sahagún, Tecciztecatl was one of the two gods who sacrificed themselves in a bonfire so that the world could continue to exist. It took Tecciztecatl several tries before he accomplished his sacrifice. Although he turned back from the heat of the fire four times, he finally made it on the fifth attempt and his sacrifice saved the world and transformed him into the Moon. The other god turned into the Sun.[3]

Cimi, the Maya word for this day, comes from the root word for "death." The glyph for the day is clearly a skull, the skull of the death god. The owl, a night bird and an omen of death, was also linked to this day, as was the underworld. Obviously, some kind of death was probably the key idea for this sign, and the skull is its symbol in both the Aztec and Maya traditions. The self-sacrifice of the god Tecciztecatl suggests the transformation of self that death brings, but it also suggests the creation of community life. The link with the Moon probably suggests the night, as does the link with the owl. One could also say that this day-sign might point to the mysteries of hell or the underworld, entered only through death.

Deer/Mazatl/Manik

This day-sign was called Mazatl and it was symbolized by the head of a deer. To the Aztecs, the deer symbolized timidity, though its patron deity was the major rain and Earth god Tlaloc, lord of all sources of water. Tlaloc, one of the principle deities of the Aztecs, was the ruler of Tlalocan, the mountain top place of the rain gods and a kind of fertile paradise. His temple was one of the two atop the major temple in the Aztec capital of Tenochtitlan.

The Maya name for this day, Manik, does not translate easily and is, unfortunately, not useful as a clue to the symbolism of this day-sign. The glyph itself, which appears to be a hand in a grasping position, is not suggestive of anything in particular either. Thompson draws some connections with the god of hunting, but this is speculation on his part.

If we consider the characteristics of the animal itself, the deer is a herd creature, timid and gentle. However, the buck or stag is nomadic, but intensely competitive and sexual during the rut. Deer are objects of a hunt and consequently a source of food, perhaps a feast as opposed to the regular diet of maize. Its connection with Tlaloc, the Earth and rain god, suggests that it may be a sign of the bounty of nature. What the glyph of the hand signifies is a mystery, though the fact that it is grasping suggests acquisition or grip. From the available evidence, the meaning of this day-sign is not particularly clear.

Rabbit/Tochtli/Lamat

Tochtli, the Aztec name for this day-sign, means rabbit. Symbolized by the head of this animal, it was regarded by the Aztecs as a tricky day. It was connected with the Lady Mayauel, the goddess of pulque, an intoxicating beverage made from the aguave plant, and was therefore connected to drunkenness. Gutierrez points out that Mayauel was the Earth-fertility goddess who lived inside the magueys, nine species of which are found on the Mexican plateau. This plant is extremely useful as a source for fibers, sharp points, fuel, and pulp for sweets, as well as liquor. As he sees it, she is a symbol for the fertility and usefulness of the Earth as well as the challenge to profit from the Earth's bounty. There are also connections between this goddess and rabbits.

The Maya equivalent of this day was called Lamat, which referred to the planet Venus, the "great star." The glyph for this day was the sign for the planet Venus itself, and in some variations is a celestial dragon with markings signifying Venus. Drunkenness is suggested by this symbolism also, because the Maya conception of Venus included the notion of a drunken person.

Rabbits are known as rapid breeders, the object of a hunt, and a source of food. The linkage with the goddess Mayuel and drunkenness, and with Venus as a drunkard, doesn't fit easily with the notion of a rabbit. But Quetzalcoatl was associated with the planet Venus and he suffered a fall from his position as a result of drinking. It is possible that what is suggested by all this is that Rabbit is the sign of over-abundance, excesses and extremes which lead to a downfall. Perhaps it is simply a symbol of Earth-fertility.

Water/Atl/Muluc

The Aztec name for this day-sign is Atl, which means water. The symbol of this day is that of a cross-section of a valley filled with water, said to suggest the passage through life. The deity linked to the sign was Xiuhtecuhtli, a fire god and the lord of time and life. Xiuhtecuhtli was the god portrayed at the center of the Earth, giving life to the entire cosmos that surrounds him in the cosmogram of the Codex Fejervary-Mayer (see Figure 7). Like water, fire was considered one of the givers of life on this planet.

The Maya name for this day was Muluc which also appears to refer water. The glyph itself is probably that of the head of a fish, though it may also refer to jade, a symbol for water, suggesting that it was precious, as well as green and blue.

Why the fire god was chosen to represent this day sign is not clear except as he symbolizes centering, the passage of time and the movement through life. Perhaps the constantly changing character of water suggested this to the Mesoamericans, or perhaps something more basic was implied, such as the life-giving properties of water. The fact that the Aztec glyph for the sign shows water in a container suggests the idea of conformity or adaptation to a fixed environment. Water takes on the shape of whatever it is placed in and it is plastic, having no real shape of its own. On the other hand, water in a channel is directed water.

Dog/Itzcuintli/Oc

Itzcuintli, which means dog, is the Aztec name for this day-sign and its symbol was that of the head of a dog. In Aztec mythology, a dog was the soul's companion as it traveled after death to Mictlan, the land of the dead. There was a belief that the dog was especially helpful in guiding its master's soul across a river in the underworld.

The deity linked to this sign was Mictlantecuhtli, lord of the souls in the underworld.

The Maya name for this day was Oc, which also means dog. In the codices, the dog is often shown holding a torch, perhaps referring to the Maya myth in which the dog brings fire to humans. Thompson links this day-sign with the Maya equivalent of the Aztec deity Xolotl, the dog-god who leads the Sun through the underworld at night. In some depictions of this day-sign, the dog's ear is emphasized, it being torn-off, mangled or diseased.

The dog, one of the most loyal of domesticated animals, was probably used to symbolize guidance, loyalty and companionship, probable themes of this sign. Why the ear of this animal came to have such importance in the glyph is not clear. Since the ear suggests alertness and the ability to guide, perhaps the damaged or maybe diseased ear is a negative suggestion of either guiding ability or sense of direction.

Monkey/Ozomatli/Chuen

Monkey is the translation of the Aztec day-sign named Ozomatli. The sign was symbolized by the head of a monkey, a figure linked to the sun god. The sign itself was said to symbolize gaiety and eroticism and those born under it were supposedly destined to become skilled artists, singers and master craftsmen. The ruling deity was Xochipilli, patron god of flowers, plants, games, singing and dancing. Known also as the "Flower Prince," this god was said to be an inspirer of dancing, drinking, and irresponsible sexual activities.

The Maya name for this day-sign was Chuen, which translates as artisan or craftsman. Among the Quiche Maya the name for this day is Batz, which is the term for monkey, particularly howling monkey. The glyphs for the sign are very stylized though some appear to show the head of a monkey. Like the Aztecs, the Maya linked this sign with the arts and the crafts.

The monkey may be a very apt symbol for the cleverness required to produce a work of art. These animals are, of course, extremely intelligent, communicative, and capable of feats well beyond those of other animals. Anyone who has watched monkeys in a zoo will understand the connection between this sign and sexuality.

Grass/Malinalli/Eb

The Aztec name for this day-sign is Malinalli which refers to a type of grass used to make sacks and cords, but translated literally, means "twisted." Another translation suggests that the word means "broom" or "brush," tools made from a dried grass. The sign was depicted by a jawbone or a skull from which vegetation sprouts. The grass symbolized was also used for blood offerings and was passed through a hole made in the tongue. It suggested sorrow and pain, and was associated with the deity Patecatl, the god of medicine and surgery.

Eb is the Maya name for this sign and it also does not translate easily. The glyph combines the symbols for death and water, which led Thompson to conclude that it symbolized harmful rains and mildew. E, the Quiche Maya name, means tooth, and in their tradition the day is considered favorable for getting good advice and for praying.

It is not easy to place these divergent ideas under one roof. Grass is a plant that has many uses, and it renews itself each year, but the linkage with death and bad rains is not clear. Perhaps, due to the connection with Patecatl, it was a sign of illness, which could lead to death. This deity also suggests the possibility of healing, the overcoming of the bad side of nature.

Reed/Acatl/Ben

Reed (Acatl to the Aztecs) refers to some type of standing vegetation which may be the reed that was used for making war darts and arrows. The sign was symbolized by the end of an arrow shaft with feathering. The warrior god Tezcatlipoca, associated with this sign, was a powerful magician considered to be one of the controlling spirits of the rhythm of the 20-day period. This god was the counterpart to Quetzalcoatl and represented the power of the dark side of existence. Together, they were the first sons of the dual creator god.

To the Maya, this day appears to have symbolized the development of both the maize plant and man. The word for the day-sign, Ben, does not seem to refer to anything in particular, plant or deity. Thompson thought that the sign probably referred to the standing corn stalk, as opposed to the ripe corn, or perhaps a reed or cane. The glyph is highly stylized, though in some variants there may be a link with vegetation. Seler believes that the glyph refers to a mat made of reeds, a kind of weaving.

Perhaps what is meant by this sign is strength and integrity, a feature shared by both a cornstalk and a war dart. The association with the god Tezcatlipoca suggests the consciousness of a warrior, a strong intent, and sense of direction.

Ocelot/Ocelotl/Ix

Ocelotl, the Aztec name for this day-sign, is one of the few Nahuatl words in the English vocabulary (others are coyotl/coyote and tomatl/tomato). It refers to the animal of its name, a jaguar or American tiger. The symbol for this day-sign is the head of a jaguar, including the depiction of its spots. Aztec lore connected the howling of the Ocelot with the passing away of darkness and the coming of sunrise. The Aztec Ocelot warriors were the spies and intelligence gatherers, and like the animal from whom they took their name, worked in the dark. Tlazolteotl, the lady of filth, was the deity linked to this day. This witch- goddess was a consumer of human evil, the one to whom sins were confessed.

The Maya name for this day, Ix, may refer to the earth god or to a magician. The Quiche Maya name, Balam, definitely means jaguar throughout the Mayan region. The connection here is that the jaguar is an animal of the underworld, of the Earth. The Maya glyph is stylized, but it appears to show the spots of this animal.

The day-sign Ocelot was probably a symbol of darkness and stealth, much like the characteristics of the animal itself. Ocelots are fierce and very dangerous creatures of the night. Their feeding habits (often capturing and eating sick or injured prey) could be a link with Tlazolteotl, the eater of filth. But she is also an Earth goddess, and ocelots were symbols of the earth suggesting a link to the regenerative function of the earth itself.

Eagle/Cuauhtli/Men

The Aztec name for this day is Cuauhtli, which means eagle. Along with its jaguar warriors, the Aztec military had eagle warriors who fought openly and directly. This day-sign was symbolized by the mask of a human face that had been skinned, or by a torn out eye, which, presumably, symbolized the extreme pain of sacrifice. The deity was Xipe Totec, the flayed god of the corn seed, a symbol of sacrifice and renewed life. This deity had some rather gruesome sacrificial rituals connected with it, suggested by the symbol for this day-sign.

The Maya called this day Men, the root word for the verb "to make" or "to do." The glyph for the day is that of a head with dots in a line behind the eyes, which Thompson regarded as evidence that the sign represented the old moon deity. The Zapotec name for the day translates as "mother" or female animal. Seler suggested that the link between these concepts was to be found in the depiction of the great mother of the gods. She is drawn with a headdress and shield of eagle feathers. An eagle's claw is also her symbol. This Maya goddess was the patroness of weaving and other female activities.

Once again, the symbolism is not consistent and the ruling deity does not shed much light on the matter. Taking the animal symbolism literally, Eagle appears to be a day-sign of high flights, great power and strength. The Aztecs regarded the eagle as a symbol for the Sun, actually the carrier of sacrificed hearts to the Sun. Xipe Totec was a god of vegetation, specifically the renewal of vegetation, though he was also a god of war. The link here might be in the idea of the "transference of energy," but this doesn't relate easily to the aged mother goddess of the Maya.

Vulture/Cozcacuauhtli/Cib

Cozcacuauhtli is the Aztec name for this day-sign and it translates as "ringed eagle," or vulture; the ring referring to the collar on this bird's neck. The sign was depicted by the head of a vulture or buzzard. To the Aztecs, vulture symbolized riches, but the ruling deity, Itzpapalotl, was the spirit of ultimate evil. She was a beautiful black stone goddess who terrified people in their dreams; the " Obsidian Butterfly." Itzpapalotl was one of the Tzitzimime, strange space creatures who were said to fall to earth from the four quarters during eclipses and eat humans.

This day-sign, called Cib by the Maya, appears to refer to a small insect, possibly the bee. The link to the Tzitzimime may be found in that the bacabs (the personified four directions in Maya cosmology) were beekeepers. Further support for this connection is the general belief that the dead return to the earth in the form of insects. The glyph itself probably represents a shell, a symbol worn by some of the Bacabs. There are jaguar features in some of the glyphs as well, suggesting darkness and night -- the time of the descent of the Tzitzimime.

Vultures are powerful birds who consume dead bodies. Perhaps what was intimated by this and the Maya link to insects was the notion of the descent of the dead and the fear that this aroused among the living. Itzpapalotl suggests negative energy in the sleeping mind, or perhaps the unconscious mind, and the Tzitzimime may be like witches.

Earthquake or Movement/Ollin/Caban

Ollin is the Aztec name for this day-sign and it translates as movement, rolling motion, or earthquake. Probably because this day-sign gave its name to the present age (the age of 4-Ollin), and because the sun god Tonatiuh appears in the center of its glyph in the Aztec Piedra del Sol, it has been linked to both the number four and the Sun. The symbol for this sign, which looks like a bow with an eye in the center, may indicate the Sun on the horizon. This symbol is also used in the codices to indicated earthquakes. The day was associated with the evil qualities of the planet Venus in its evening star phase, the negative aspect of Quetzalcoatl. The ruling deity was Xolotl, a monstrous animal god, terrible and unhappy, who brought the Sun down in the west at night.

The Maya name for this day was Caban which means Earth, and there are associations of this day with earthquakes. The Maya glyph of the day has a curving line which may represent the lock of hair of the young Moon goddess, who is also the goddess of the Earth. The Maya considered this day good for matchmaking, medicine, and commerce.

Gutierrez interprets Earthquake or Movement as the day-sign of the perpetual activity of the universe. He also translates Xolotl to mean "companion" rather than "monstrous" or "deformed." This might explain the connection with matchmaking, but it doesn't relate directly to earthquakes. In this text, and in many of my other writings, I have more frequently referred to this sign as Earthquake, although the name Motion may be a more appropriate translation.

Knife/Tecpatl/Etz'nab

The name for this day-sign comes from the Aztec name Tecpatl which means "flint stone" or "flint knife." The symbol here is that of the sacrificial knife, the flint knife used to remove the hearts from sacrificial victims. Tezcatlipoca, in his form as Chalchiuhtotolin, the "Jeweled Turkey," was the Aztec deity. Like the legends concerning this deity, this day-sign was considered both lucky or unlucky; a bold man could seize the moment if he willed it.

The Maya name was Etz'nab which also translates as something like "knife" or "sharp implement." The glyph for the sign appears to indicate a blade and the same design is frequently found on the tips of spears where they are depicted.

Most likely, this day-sign signified decisiveness. Knife, as the yearbearer of the north for the Aztecs, was considered barren and cold. Gutierrez writes that the association with the jeweled- turkey aspect of Tezcatlipoca is the key to this sign. The turkey is a symbol of vanity and, according to him, that is precisely what the sign emphasizes.

Rain/Quiahuitl/Cauac

Quiahuitl is the Aztec name for this day-sign. It was symbolized by Tlaloc, the rain god, but the ruling deity was Tonatiuh, the sun god, whose face appears in the center of the Aztec Sun Stone or Piedra del Sol. As a sun-god, one would expect Tonatiuh to be a provider of light and life. Some sources say the hearth goddess Chantico rules this sign.[4]

The Maya name for this day was Cauac, which translates as "storm," "thunder," and "rain." The glyph appears to contain clouds and symbols that also appear on drawings of the celestial dragons, which bring rains and storms. The Guatamalan name for this day, Ayotl, means "turtle." There is a link with rain here as this animal, as well as the frog, are depicted as coming down with the rain.

Rain appears to be a day-sign of resources from the sky, as opposed to ground water. Water, as a life-giving substance, suggests something around which people gather. The Sun would serve a similar function.

Flower/Xochitl/Ahau

Xochitl, which means "flower," is the Aztec name for this day-sign. The symbol clearly represents a flower, which in itself was a symbol of perfection and beauty. Xochiquetzal, the goddess of the underworld, symbolized by the temporary beauty of the flower, was the ruling deity.

The Maya name for this day-sign was Ahau, which means "lord" or "chief." The glyph for the day is sometimes a four petaled flower though it also appears as a face. To the Maya, the flower was a symbol of the Lord or Sun, and this was its day.

This day-sign was a symbol for the perfection of the Sun, revealed in the flower. The perfection of both may be the common link, and this perfection may be something to worship. This last of the twenty named days concludes a sequence which began with the creation of the world. In Maya calendrics, it is this sign that completes or finishes a katun cycle and gives its name to it. In other words, the Maya named each katun cycle for its last day which was the day Ahau. Perhaps the flower, the highest form and perfection (lord) of a plant, and also a product of the Sun (lord), is a fitting ending to this string of symbols.

It is obvious from the above attempts to piece together the sometimes common, sometimes divergent, symbolism of the days-signs that much has been lost since Classic Mayan and even Aztec times. Besides the names of the days, the symbols, and the associated deities, some descriptions of character types has come down to us from Durán's writings. In his book on the calendar, he reports the "fates of the signs," as told to him from native informants. According to Durán, the day-signs were either good, neutral, or bad for those born under them. The good signs were Crocodile, House, Lizard, Deer, and Vulture. The neutral ones, which were changeable and subject to both good and bad fortune, were Rabbit, Monkey, Reed, Jaguar, Eagle, Earthquake, and Flower. The "evil, ill-omened" signs were Wind, Serpent, Death, Water, Grass, Knife, and Rain. Below are brief descriptions of the "fates" of the signs, or how a person born under a particular day-sign would be described, according to Durán.[5]

Crocodile/Alligator: People born under this sign would be strong, courageous, hard workers, and famous warriors. They would be very busy, efficient, and honest people as well.

Wind: This was the day when erratic, fickle, and lazy persons were born.   These people were said to be addicted to merrymaking, overindulgent, and without roots.

House: Those born under it were seclusive, peaceful, respectful and inclined to stay at home. They had peaceful deaths.

Lizard: This one produced fortunate persons who were outstanding in their family and came to possess wealth, without having to work too hard for it.

Serpent: Persons born on this day were to become poor, dependent, and lacking in clothes.
Death: Persons who are sad, depressed, weak-hearted, sickly, etc.

Deer: Woodsmen, hunters, runners, walkers, and travelers.

Rabbit: The description is said to be the same as for Deer.

Water: Persons who are ill, apathetic, and sufferers. Always discontented and angry, they live short lives.

Dog: Courageous and generous persons who have many children. They had lives of bliss and felicity.

Monkey: Actors and singers who made their living from their cleverness. They have many friends and if female, are easily persuaded

Grass: Persons born under this sign were doomed to become sick every year, though they do not die from this cycle of illness.

Reed: Men without heart, hollow and incompetent. They were unwise, beggars, and addicted to idleness, lying in the sun naked.

Ocelot: Daring, conceited and courageous persons who are eager for honor and position. Willing to fight for any cause and do whatever is necessary to improve their position.

Eagle: Same nature as jaguar except for addictions to theft and envy of other's wealth.

Vulture: These persons lived long, were strong, free of disease, authoritative, muscular, and bald. They were wise, good advisors and teachers.

Earthquake/Movement: Blessed, fortunate and successful, if male. If female, rich and prosperous, but stupid and confused.

Knife: Persons who are harsh, cold, sinful, and sterile. They were fortunate in many other ways, however.

Rain: An ill-omened sign of sickness, blindness, lameness and insanity.

Flower: Painters, weavers, sculptors, and other workers of the arts.
Women who were skilled in the decorative arts, clean, and diligent.

In addition to the writings of the friars, there are character
descriptions of the twenty days that survive as an oral tradition in
parts of Mexico and Guatamala. Many towns have maintained the
260-day count since the Conquest without dropping a day. Anthro-
pologist Barbara Tedlock became an initiated daykeeper, or calendar
diviner, among the Quiche Maya and has written on the contemporary use and meanings of the twenty named days.[6]   While the
Quiche names for the day-signs differ to some extent from the Classic
Maya, they follow the same sequence. From the standpoint of word
associations,   links between the words, their sounds, and their
meanings, it is apparent that their calendar is the same as that of the
Classic Maya, but has become stylized and adapted to their own
particular cultural level and needs.

One difference between the Quiche Maya and the Classic Maya is
in regard to the starting day, the first day of the count. Throughout
pre-Conquest Mexico and Central America, the list of the twenty
named days usually began with the day-sign Imix/Crocodile. There
were exceptions, for example the Nicaraguan count began with
Ben/Reed, but it followed the same order from that starting point. In
her work on Quiche Maya calendar divination, Tedlock reports that
her informants did not regard any of the days as the p73 start of the
count, it was a continuous sequence with no beginning or end. When
pressed, they did point to the day 8-Batz (8- Monkey) as a day of
particular importance, as that was a day for important ceremonies.

In Tedlock's account of Quiche Maya delineations of the day-
signs, she points out the importance of the mnemonics for each name.
Apparently, there are a number of associations for each name that are
not directly connected to its basic meaning. Knowing these "memory
pegs" assists in delineating the day-signs. The mnemonics themselves
aren't really delineations, yet they hint in the direction that
interpretations should go. In the Quiche delineations listed in
Tedlock's book there are constant references as to whether or not the
person will become a calendar- diviner or priest-shaman. It appears

that these character descriptions are ones that would be useful to the calendar-diviners themselves, and as such represent a body of knowledge specific to that region. There is also an emphasis on the good or bad fortune associated with each day, something obviously needed in divination.

Chapter 5

The Tonalamatl or Book of Fate

In many of the approximately twenty or so surviving picture books painted before or shortly after the Spanish Conquest, are complex listings and depictions of the twenty named days in the 260-day astrological calendar. In Aztec times these books were named tonalamatl, literally "book of days" or "book of fate." The word "tonal" refers to warmth, Sun and day, the ending "amatl" refers to book or paper.[1] These books were kept in the temples and consulted by both priests and specialists in divination. Like the Western zodiac, where the twelve signs are divided and organized by element and quality, the 260-day count was also apportioned in some very interesting and symmetrical ways.

Of the several surviving codices concerned with the sacred calendar, the Codex Borgia is perhaps the best illustrated. It is a pre-Conquest document that probably comes from somewhere within the Aztec empire, possibly the Mixtec region near Oaxaca. In it, the order of the days, their deities, and their relationships to the four directions are depicted, along with other more complex rulership patterns. The Codex Vaticanus B is also from this region and period, though its artwork is cruder than the Borgia. The other codices that elaborate upon the 260-day count are the Codex Laud, the Codex Fejervary-Mayer, the Codex Cospiano, Codex Borbonicus, and the Tonalamatl of the Aubin Collection. Among the Maya codices, the Dresden is primarily astronomical, but the Madrid contains much astrological symbolism including a prognosticatory almanac.[2]

One of the outstanding characteristics of these codices is in the full listing of the 260 days. While there are some variations between codices, the basic layout of the calendar is in twenty segments of thirteen. Crocodile or Alligator begins the sequence and is numbered

one. Wind comes next, numbered two, House is three, etc. When
Reed is reached, at number thirteen, the next day-sign, Jaguar, begins
the count again with the number one. These are the trecena that
appear to have been considered extremely important in evaluating a
birth or an event.

Not much has been written about these tonalamatl, in part due to
the inherent difficulties involved in learning a pictorial or
hieroglyphic language, and in part due to the distaste of the academic
researcher for anything astrological. Segments of the codices have
been used in texts to illustrate books on ancient Mexico, but aside
from Seler's early work, they remain for the most part ignored and
unexplored. An examination of one of these documents reveals the
variety of symbolic interpretations of any one day in the 260-day
calendar. Each day-sign, which is a symbol in itself and connected to
one of the directions, has a number from one to thirteen attached to it,
is contained within a trecena of thirteen days and is located, along
with 65 other days, within one of the four Tonalamatl quarters
designated by compass direction (see Appendix B). But this is not all
that is contained within one of these documents. There are more
complex directional schemes including the order of the nine Lords of
the Night (discussed later) and the thirteen Day Lords and Birds. One
gets the impression that only a trained person in these matters could
perceive and interpret the subtle differences between days, hardly the
kind of thinking that academics are inclined toward.

The Tonalamatl of the Codex Vaticanus B, which is similar in
design to the Borgia, illustrates the basic arrangement of the 260 days
in four long columns of five day-signs. Seler calls this "the
Tonalamatl disposed of in columns of five members." On the first
page, 1-Crocodile begins the listing at the lower left- hand corner.
Reading left to right, this list ends with 13-Reed at the lower right-
hand side of the page. On the next line, above the 1-Crocodile
column, 1-Reed begins a thirteen sign sequence. Above this is 1-
Serpent, then 1-Earthquake and, on the top, 1-Water. The numbers
of the columns remain constant, one through thirteen, and there are
images of gods and other things above and below each column. This
first page of the tonalamatl is called its first quarter which is the
region of the east. Note that the five day-signs that head the list on

the left, those with the number one, are all signs of the east as described in a previous chapter.

On the second page of the tonalamatl, the listing again begins at the lower left-hand column with the day 1-Jaguar. This continues the natural order of the twenty named days from the lowest column of the previous page. Reed, the last day-sign of the lowest listing on the first page is always followed by Jaguar, here the numbering places them on separate pages. Further, all the leading day-signs of this second page, those with the number one attached and standing in the first column on the left, are signs of the north. These are Jaguar, Death, Knife, Dog and Wind.

The same pattern is followed for the next page which starts with the western signs, Deer, Rain, Monkey, House and Eagle, and the fourth page of the southern signs, Flower, Grass, Lizard, Vulture, and Rabbit. In just four pages of listings, the entire 260-day sequence is presented with its numbers, directions and other symbolic information. The Codex Borgia differs from the Codex Vaticanus B in that the listing is read from right to left, although both read from down to up. The tonalamatl I created for Appendix B maintains the true form of the Borgia and Vaticanus B but arranges the material so that it reads from left to right and up to down, making it easier for Westerners to read.

In many respects, the arrangement reminds one of the I-Ching where a series of 64 hexagrams can be arranged in at least two different ways, and where placements are related to the directions and the seasons. It could be said that the tonalamatl is Mesoamerica's I-Ching, an attempt to locate the order of the universe and make it intelligible to men. Jose Arguelles has called the 260 day calendar the "harmonic module," a reference to its beauty, symmetry and capsule description of the cosmos.[3] This is an interesting name for the sacred calendar and certainly easier to pronounce than the Nahuatl words tonalpouhalli or Tonalamatl. It also conveys the sense that this unit can be used with any sequence of time periods, which, as we will see in later chapters, it can.

In the tonalamatl, illustrations appear above and below each column of five named days. In the Codex Vaticanus B, the first column where 1-Crocodile, 1-Reed, 1-Earthquake and 1-Water are stacked atop each other, a drawing which Seler calls "the descent of the offerings" appears above, and one of Quetzalcoatl appears below. In the next column, the two's, a drawing of a priest appears above, and below is a drawing of two snakes. One immediately is inclined to read this as an indication of some further sub-rulership scheme, but the various tonalamatls are not consistent in the placement or even nature of these drawings, although the Borgia comes very close to the Vaticanus B. Seler came to the conclusion that the drawing immediately under the first column, in all the manuscripts, is constant and does relate to the compass direction of the page, but the others are probably mere decoration of some sort. Besides Quetzalcoatl in the east, the tonalamatls have Tezcatlipoca in the north, an Earth goddess in the west and Tonatiuh, the Sun god, in the south.

The 13-Day Periods

Another common tonalamatl arrangement found in the codices is a listing of each of the 13-day periods on a page with the appropriate rulers of the period. A good example is found in the Codex Borbonicus in which the 13 days of each trecena are individually listed with accompanying diurnal ruler, nocturnal ruler, and bird. A large part of the page is devoted to the ruling deity of the trecena and other relevant symbols of the period. The day lord, nocturnal lord and bird rulers designate each of the 13 days themselves that make up one trecena. This type of tonalamatl is twenty pages long.

While the interpretations of each of the days or trecenas as shown in the tonalamatl of the various codices remains in part a mystery, Sahagun, the great collector of Aztec lore, did record some meanings of the twenty 13-day weeks. In Books Four and Five of the Florentine Codex, entitled the "The Soothsayers and the Omens," are found descriptions, some in great detail, of each of the twenty trecena or 13-day periods. As we have seen from the tonalamatl, each period is composed of thirteen days, numbered in the order of the day-signs from the one that begins the series. In Sahagun's descriptions, he included, for the first few periods, individual variations for each number and day combination. He probably became tired of this and omitted delineations for the last seven periods, although he did make it clear that, in general, the third, seventh, and tenth through thirteenth days were good, the others bad.

Below are listed the fates of the 13-day periods ruled by the first of each of the 20 named days according to Sahagun.[4] Within each period are thirteen numbered days, each of which had a specific fate within the general context of the period. For example, the 3rd day of the 13-day period 1-Deer was the day 3- Water. The individual day, in this case 3-Water, had its fate, but within the overall rulership of the week 1-Deer. This might be compared to the Western astrological notion of the decans and the dwadamshas (dwads), subdivisions of the twelve principal signs. Readers steeped in Western humanistic astrology who find the negativity in the friar's delineations appalling should be reminded that his intention was to eradicate the system, not to preserve it.

1-Crocodile or Alligator: This 13-day period promised wealth or fortunate conditions in life, though some effort would be needed to overcome defects.   It was a favorable period for beginnings, and it gave outstanding courage and strength. All of the days of this period blessed.

1-Ocelot: This day, not the full 13-day period, was considered unfortunate. Those born here would die in war, become captives or slaves, and become adulterous.   It made one daring, prideful selfish, and ambitious. Women born on the day 1-Ocelot were said to be like wild beasts; adulterers and miserable. Fortunately, this description only applied to the day 1-Ocelot itself. Sahagun does not mention the second and third days of the week, 2- Eagle and 3-Vulture, but he does note that 4-Earthquake/Movement was considered an important day, the day of the Sun. Of course, this was the day that the present age, depicted on the Aztec Calendar Stone, was named after. The day 7-Flower is mentioned as being both good and bad, and also 9-Wind, as an evil day, a day of losses.

1-Deer: This was a fortunate day on which to be born, but, unfortunately, all could be lost due to laziness. Those born then would be well-liked but fearful, particularly of lightning. Sahagun goes on for pages about the second day of this week, 2- Rabbit, which apparently produced drunkards. The extremely long and detailed description of the depravity and perversion that this day-sign was known for leads one to wonder what the good friar was really interested in. 3-Water gave riches that would vanish, 4-Dog favored the breeding of dogs, and 5-Monkey produced comedians and entertainers. A "day of wild beasts" was 6-Grass, but 7-Reed was good and destined to riches. The next four days were without merit but 13-Rain was fortunate and led to wealth and a long life.

1-Flower: Those born under this 13-day period would be happy, able and entertaining. Women born here would become great embroiders. However, one's fate depended on commitment to the highest principles of the sign itself. Those who failed became conceited artists and ended in ruin. Sahagun does not say anything about the other days in this week except that some were good and some bad.

1-Reed: This was considered a generally unfortunate period, especially the 9th day, the day 9-Crocodile. The sign supposedly produced bad characters, incompetents, liars, and lazy persons incapable of keeping secrets. The first six days of the period were to be avoided for baptisms, the day 7-Rain being far more desirable for such an important ritual. 8-Flower was also considered favorable, but 9-Crocodile was perverse and full of vice. The last four days, 10-Wind, 11-House, 12-Lizard and 13-Serpent were better and made one rich and honorable.

1-Death: Those born on the first day of this 13-day period, the day 1-Death, would become rich and would prosper. It was a favorable day for slaves who were treated well and in some cases achieved glory and honor. 2-Deer was an evil and miserable day, a day when cowards were born. 3-Rabbit was good, but those born under it had enigmatic eating habits. 4-Water was another miserable day that suggested a life of struggle. 5-Dog was evil and so was 6-Monkey. 7-Grass was considered favorable enough for a baptism which had skipped the previous days, but 8-Reed and 9- Ocelot were bad "days of wild beasts." 10-Eagle was good, those born under it were brave and strong and inspiring warriors. 11- Vulture produced persons who lived long but become bent with age. 12-Earthquake/Movement and 13-Knife were favorable.

1-Rain: This 13-day period was mostly unfortunate and its influence disastrous. It caused bad luck and illness. The third day, 3-Crocodile, produced astrologers and sorcerers who could change themselves into animals.   4-Wind was indifferent -- it was consecrated to the execution of adulterers, yet favored by the merchants and was a day for them to display their wares. 5-House and 6-Lizard produced those of hot temper; 7-Serpent promised riches and merit. 8-Death was evil and 9-Deer also, it producing those given to vice and sin. 10-Rabbit, however, was considered a very good day in this mostly terrible week. One born on this day would receive great gifts and riches. But apparently due to the favorable qualities on the next three days, one born on 10- Rabbit would be baptized on 13-Monkey, the last day of the week. Sahagun reports that was a way of greatly strengthening the day and improving it.

1-Grass: Generally this was considered an evil, unhealthy and dark period. Those born here had chronic annual illnesses. The sign gave one at first a good chance but this was followed by misfortune. It promised many children who would die. 2-Reed and 3-Ocelot were considered better than the first day.   4-Eagle, 5- Vulture and 6-Movement were bad days, birthdays of those who lived in vice and misery. 7-Knife was fortunate, but 8-Rain and 9-Flower were days of thieves and adulterers.

1-Serpent: In general, this was a good day. Persons born under it would come to be wealthy, but could also fall to ruin if they were neglectful. It was an important and favorable period for merchants and traders to begin journeys, and also for soldiers to go to war. 2-Death, which followed it, was evil, 3-Deer was good, 4-Rabbit and 5-Water were evil, and 6-Dog was the birthday of sickly and weak persons who were constantly suffering. 7- Monkey was a good day to be born on and produced those with good social skills. 8-Grass was good, but 9-Reed was a day when haughty and vicious persons were born.   10-Ocelot was good, 11- Eagle and 12-Vulture indifferent, and 13-Movement the best of the series.

1-Knife: One born on this day would be a valiant leader who would gain riches and honor if a man, and would be extremely competent and skillful if a woman. The rest of the days of this week were all considered favorable and fortunate.

1-Monkey: This 13-day period was said to produce singers, dancers, and painters; those who were talented, popular and sociable. Unfortunately, those who fell ill during this sign could not be cured. 2-Grass was not a good day, those born under it would produce many sons, but all would die. The rest of the days followed the same general pattern -- the third, seventh, and tenth through thirteenth being good, the others bad.

1-Lizard: Those born on this day became prosperous without effort. This was a good sign, producing strong and agile persons, capable of surviving falls. Sahagun says little about the other days except that 4-Deer, 5-Rabbit, and 6-Water were unfavorable.

1-Earthquake/Movement: This day gave success to those who did their penances. Those who did not take heed would experience misery and become vagabonds. The rest of the days in this 13-day period were considered favorable.

1-Dog: This period was regarded as fortunate and it produced persons who became rich and owners of many slaves. (From here on, Sahagun does not discuss in detail any individual days except for the first. He reminds the reader that the days which follow the first of any sign conformed to the general pattern noted previously.)

1-House: This was considered a very unfortunate day that produced vice, sin and even tortuous death. It was the sign of adulterers, slaves and robbers. Women were liars, vain and often ended up being sacrificed. Positively, it made one reclusive. Anyone born on this day was baptized on 3-Serpent or 7-Water, which could improve conditions somewhat.

1-Vulture: If one survived, this was a fortunate day that gave wisdom, long life and happiness. However, many persons born on this day would die early. The rest of the week followed the usual pattern.

1-Water: This was an evil day that brought little joy early in life and none later on. Persons born on this day would eventually become evil and would meet a sad death. Death could possibly come from being crushed by stones, or perhaps drowning. There was a very slim chance, however, that such a person would temporarily receive some reward. If one were a merchant, it was said that his goods would be swept away by a river. The rest of the week was as usual.

1-Wind: This day was unfortunate and produced astrologers and sorcerers who took the form of animals. If the person was a noble, he would become a traitor. It made one restless, fickle, lazy, and subject to possession. No comment on the other days.

1-Eagle: An unfortunate day producing rash, presumptuous slanderers and those addicted to theft. Men born under this sign became leaders but they respected no one. They pretended to be virtuous but saw no virtue in others. Women born on this day were shameless, immodest, and of evil tongue. They derived great pleasure from speaking evil and beating on other persons.

1-Rabbit: This was a very fortunate day and promised prosperity and acquired riches to those who worked for them. This was a sign that produced those who tried everything and were successful, never being defrauded nor experiencing loss through mismanagement. These were very busy people who also took to traveling. On the other hand, such persons were easily frightened.

The notion of the 13-day periods is also found in the codices, particularly the Codex Borbonicus and the Codex Telleriano-Remenis. These manuscripts clearly associate particular deities with each period, similar in concept to the rulership of a god over each day. The rulerships are as follows:

1. Crocodile: Tonacatecuhtli-Tonacacihuatl -- creator duality
2. Ocelot: Quetzalcoatl -- feathered serpent and wind god
3. Deer: Tepeyollotl -- jaguar god, interior earth god
4. Flower: Ueuecoyotl -- old dance god
5. Reed: Chalchihuitlicue -- goddess of ground water and storms
6. Death: Tecciztecatl -- sacrificed Moon god
7. Rain: Tlaloc -- rain god
8. Grass: Mayauel -- goddess of pulque
9. Serpent: Xiuhtecuhtli -- fire god, and Tlahuizcalpantecuhtli
10. Knife: Mictlantecuhtli -- god of underworld
11. Monkey: Patecatl -- god of medicine
12. Lizard: Ixtlacoliuhqui -- god of ice and punishment
13. Earthquake/Movement: Tlazolteotl -- Earth goddess of filth
14. Dog: Xipe Totec -- flayed god
15. House: Itzapapalotl -- obsidian butterfly
16. Vulture: Xolotl -- god of underworld, Evening Star
17. Water: Chalchiuhtotolin -- Tezcatlipoca as "jeweled turkey"
18. Wind: Chantico -- hearth goddess
19. Eagle: Xochiquetzal -- flower goddess
20. Rabbit: Iztapatotec -- Xiuhtecuhtli -- fire and sacrifice god

When one compares this order of deities to that of the order of the twenty day-signs (see the beginning of Chapter 4), one is struck by the fact that the first ten gods (not the day names) are exactly the same in both lists. Also, the rulership order from number 13, Tlazolteotl, to number 19, Xochiquetzal, is consistent with the day-order but one place behind. There are also some additional deities, not found in the rulership of the twenty days, that are found in this secondary order. Seler notes the striking correlations and displacements between the two rulerships lists and comments that it is the eleventh sign, which should be Xochipilli, that the shift occurs. Xochipilli is omitted, the next nine deities are moved up and Xiuhtecutli is added to complete the sequence. Seler does not find any specific reason or motive for this, and he makes no further comment.

C.A. Burland notes that this series of 20 signs or weeks of thirteen days reveals an inner order corresponding to the five principal directions of Mesoamerican cosmology.[5] For the Aztecs the East was considered the direction of beginnings, presumably because this was where the Sun rose each morning. The first four trecena may belong to this direction because the ruling deities have associations that pertain to the theme of emergence.

Alligator - Ometecuhtli, the lord of life and creation.
Ocelot - Quetzalcoatl, god of the morning star.
Deer - Tepeyollotl, god of the sunrise.
Flower - Ueuecoyotl, god of emergence to consciousness.

The south was considered the region of fertility and growth.
Reed - Chalchihuitlicue, goddess of water and storms.
Death - Tecciztecatl, the old Moon god.
Rain - Tlaloc, lord of all sources of water.
Grass - Mayauel, goddess of intoxicating pulque.

The north was associated with mystery and the unknown.
Serpent - Xiuhtecuhtli, lord of fire from hearth to pole star.
Knife - Mictlantecuhtli, lord of the region of the dead.
Monkey - Patecatl, lord of medicines.
Lizard - Itzcoliuhqui, lord of cold and terrifying things.

The west was the place of the sunset and endings.
Earthquake - Tlazolteotl, goddess who takes the sun down.
Dog - Xipe Totec, god of burial and resurrection.
House - Itzpapalotl, the terror of approaching darkness.
Vulture - Xolotl, the deep unconscious which swallows memory.

The center or middle earth was the fifth direction, a point of centrality, focus and source.
Water - Tezcatlipoca, god of warriors.
Wind - Chantico, goddess of hearth in the home.
Eagle - Xochiquetzal, goddess of the beauty of the underworld.
Rabbit - Xiuhtecuhtli, lord of central fire.

Burland's grouping of the day-signs in fours and their assignment to all four directions plus the center direction is supported, to some extent, by cosmograms such as that in the Codex Fejevery- Mayer. In these, the center is as important a direction as the four quarters. Still, the Tonalamatl in columns of five does not seem to support this particular five-fold division. The five day-signs on the first page are all signs of the east according to the basic directional arrangement, not the first four of the secondary sequence of signs (see Appendix C). The gods listed above appear to support Burland's idea, but the arrangement is not completely convincing. In the opinion of this author, something is amiss here. The rulerships of the 13-day periods are too close to the original rulerships. Quite possibly the manuscripts with these rulerships are incorrect or sloppy copies of originals. The parallels between the two orders are too close and the errors not great enough to suggest that this linkage with deities indicates a separate and distinct kind of rulership.

More likely, the rulerships follow the same pattern, as in the Greco-Roman decans or the dwadashamsas of Hindu astrology.[6] In both of these systems, the signs are broken down into fractions, ten degrees for the decans and two and one half degrees for the dwadashamsas. Each segment then takes on the characteristic of the zodiacal sign it corresponds to in the order of the signs. For example, the third decan or third ten-degree segment of the zodiac corresponds to the third sign Gemini, even though this ten-degree segment is located in the sign Aries. Likewise, the third dwadashamsa of any sign corresponds to the third sign, Gemini. The decan or dwadashamsa *modifies the sign it is located within by bringing in the influence of another sign.* If this analogy is correct, then the order of ruling gods in the primary twenty day sequence would be applied to the order of the 13-day periods and indicate a kind of sub-influence. For example, the twelfth trecena (1-Lizard) would be ruled by the god of the twelfth day-sign (Grass), which is Patecatl.

The Burner Periods

The tonalamatl is normally divided into four 65-day sections, each assigned to one of the four directions. The order of the day-signs is normally listed in 13 rows and in columns of five. This quartering of the 260-day astrological calendar is also reflected in ritual sequences recorded by the Maya as the burner periods. In some of the Books of Chilam Balam, these ritual periods are noted alongside listings of the 260 days.[7] Words translated as "the burner takes the fire" are written opposite the days 3-Chicchan (Serpent), 3-Oc (Dog), 3-Men (Eagle), and 3- Ahau (Flower). Alongside 10 Chicchan, 10-Oc, 10-Men, and 10-Ahau is "the burner fire begins, or flares up." At 4-Chicchan, 4-Oc, 4-Men, and 4-Ahau is "the fire of the burner runs." These days are the actual burners themselves. Finally, at 11-Chicchan, 11- Oc, 11-Men, and 11-Ahau "the burner extinguishes the fire." Since each of the same day-signs in the 260-day count are spaced 20 days apart, the entire sequence from the taking to the extinguishing of the fire lasts for 60 days. But from the taking of the fire to the next taking of the fire, for example from 3- Chicchan to 3-Oc is 65 days, one quarter of 260. Exactly what the purpose or rituals of the burner periods is unclear. Thompson lists a number of possibilities, including rain-making rituals or even fire-walking ceremonies, but the matter is by no means clear and settled.

The idea of dividing up the 260-day calendar, as if it were a circle, into halves and fourths, fifths and possibly even further segments, appears in the burner periods of the Maya and also in the various tabulations of the count in the codices. A division by four will emphasize four day-signs, each representing one of the quarters or directions. This is the case with the burner periods described above, Chicchan, Oc, Men and Ahau being signs of the east, north, west and south respectively. Division by five produces five groups of 52 days, the same number of years in a calender round. This division will make five day-signs the focus, and each of these five will be ruled by the same direction. For example, division by five starting with Imix will put that sign, Ben, Chicchan, Caban and Muluc at the head of each column, all of these being the signs of the east. The 260-day count is capable of an amazing number of manipulations that bring astrology, numerology, directionology, astronomy and theology into conjunction. In this book we can only hope to scratch the surface of a very complex system.

The Lords of the Night

In the codices that contain a tonalamatl are also pictorial diagrams suggesting a host of other arrangements and linkages between the day-signs, the gods, the directions, Day Lords, trees and birds. One important sequence was that of the Lords of the Night, also known as the Nine Figures. These nine gods of the night or underworld are found in both the Maya and Aztec traditions. The glyphs of the nine Maya gods have been identified, but the names of the gods themselves are not known and they have been labeled G-1 through G-9.[8] The names of the Aztec gods in this series are well known and occupy a prominent place in the several codices that contain astrological and cosmological material.

In the frontispiece of the Codex Fejervary-Mayer the nine Lords of the Night are shown as part of the cosmic scheme (see Figure 7). As we have already seen, this remarkable diagram also displays the 13-day period arrangement of the tonalamatl and its relationships to the four directions or quarters. In the center of the diagram is the god Xiuhtecuhtli, the Lord of Central Fire. In the region of the east, above the center, are Itztli, the sacrificial knife god, and Piltzintecutli, the Sun god. In the north are Tepeyollotl, the jaguar god, and Tlaloc, the rain god. In the west are Chalchihuitlicue, the water goddess, and Tlazolteotl, the filth goddess. In the region of the south are Cinteotl, the maize god, and Mictlantecuhtli, the god of the underworld. The usual order of the nine Lords is as follows with Quiauitecuhtli, a rain god, sometimes substituted for Tlaloc.

1. Xiuhtecuhtli
2. Itzli
3. Piltzintecuhtli
4. Cinteotl
5. Mictlantecuhtli
6. Chalchiuhtlicue
7. Tlazolteotl
8. Tepeyollotl
9. Tlaloc

The actual role of the Lords is not exactly clear. In some of the codices they run concurrent in the tonalamatl with the day-signs, in others they stand alone. What is important about these gods for our study is that they do appear near or connected with the tonalamatl in several codices and seem to have some symbolic connection to the rhythms of time. Like the twenty signs and the thirteen numbers they may, therefore, be astrological in nature.

Seler, in seeking an explanation for both the number 9 and the night aspect of these gods, looked to the Moon and the fact that there are nine lunations in one 260-day period. He suggested that the nine moons of the tonalpouhalli were named after these gods and that the list and order became sacred.[9] It is also true that nine is the number of the underworld in Mesoamerican cosmology. Throughout the Mesoamerican culture region, the cosmos was conceived of as having 13 heavens above and 9 underworlds below. It is not clear whether these layers were stacked vertically (which is what some drawings suggest) or if they were arranged as a pyramid, with the center god standing at the apex or nadir.

Seler also suggested that the nine Lords of the Night were actually rulers over divisions of the night, a kind of hour system. He also thought that the day might have been divided into thirteenths. In both cases, the central deity would stand at midnight or noon and the others on either side of this position. Seler thought that the ancient astrologers would need to know the fate of the hour as well as the day, and that only with an hour system and a rulership pattern was this possible. The nine Lords of the Night would naturally be stronger in influence and more fateful than those of the day because the night is less controllable than the day. We are not sure exactly what and how the nine Lords of the Night ruled over time in the Mexican region. The cycle of 9 does not divide evenly into 260, and 9 cycles of 260-days must occur before the same day-sign and Lord rejoin. This turns out to be 2,340 days or 6.4 years. It is also true that 9 cycles of 52 years must pass before the same 365-day, 260- day and 9-day cycles meet. In the Maya region, however, the situation is more precise because the length of the symbolic year, called a tun, is 360 days, and this figure is evenly divisible by 9. Completions of tuns and katuns (20 tuns) always neatly end with the same Lord of the Night. We will see more of this in Chapter 7.

All that is known for sure about the Lords of the Night is that they were a set of major deities that had links to the the sequence of days, and the four directions and center. Maybe they were another layer of symbolism for each day in general. Maybe they were nocturnal rulers; astrological influences that primarily affected night births. This latter idea is a very real possibility because a tradition exists in Western astrology of making distinctions between night and day births. While the Maya apparently had this 9-day sequence running continuously along with the 260-day count, meeting exactly only every 9th 260-day period, the Aztec codices suggest something different. It appears that the 9- day cycle was restarted for every 260-day period, regardless of the fact that 260 is not evenly divisible by 9. This meant that two of the Lords of the Night ruled the 260th day.

In addition to the nine Lords of the Night, some of the codices list 13 day lords and 13 birds. It is probable that these were two different but overlapping sets of symbols. The Maya definitely assigned god names to the numbers, but their list went beyond thirteen. Again, whether or not this count of thirteen symbolic lords and birds were elaborations on the symbolism of the 13 numbers that cycled with the 20 day-signs is unclear. The available evidence does not indicate a set of hour rulers, as Seler suggested. More intriguing is the 20-page tonalamatl listing in the Codex Borbonicus in which the 13 days of each trecena are listed with a day lord, a nocturnal lord and a bird. Unfortunately, the list of nocturnal lords in this tonalamatl is not consistent with the usual list of the Lords of the Night and so we are left with only hints suggesting that day rulerships were probably distinguished from night rulerships. The thirteen birds are yet another level of symbolism that remains unclear.[10] However, it should be stated that a number of modern-day practitioners of Aztec astrology in Mexico do use the birds and the Lords of the Night in their work, but their calendar correlations vary and are also subject to periodic adjustments.

Brotherston (1979:85-93) organizes the symbolic cycles of the tonalamatl in a simple and direct way, which may very well be the way the system worked. In his view there are simply three main ritual sets, the Nine Figures, the Thirteen Numbers and the Twenty Signs.

The Nine Figures are the nine Lords of the Night, and the Twenty Signs are the twenty day-signs. The Thirteen Numbers include the birds and day-lords as well as the numbers. In other words, the birds and day-lords are simply descriptive symbolism of the thirteen numbers that cycle with the day-signs. Brotherston goes further and suggests that the Nine Figures represent the nine nights that transpire when Venus changes from an evening star to a morning star, a time symbolic of primary origins or parental forces. The Thirteen Numbers show luck and may be lunar in origin, and the Twenty Signs are solar. Perhaps it is that simple; Mesoamerican astrologers reduced planetary influence to numerologically significant sequences of days.

Chapter 6

Quetzalcoatl and the Planet Venus

Along with the Sun and Moon, Venus was probably studied more intensely than any of the other heavenly bodies visible to the ancient Mesoamericans. Unlike the time-period astrology of the 260-day calendar and the katun cycle, the observations and lore associated with this planet may constitute an early form of what might be called "planetary astrology."[1] Tremendous efforts were put into aligning architectural constructions in order that the movements of this planet could be tracked and recorded accurately. The Maya, in particular, were known to have excelled in such constructions and also in the preparation of tables indicating where in its cycle Venus could be found at any given time.

To the Maya, Venus - the "Great Star" - was very much a visible symbol of the ebb and flow of life. Because it orbits between the Earth and the Sun, it appears to an earthbound observer to be linked with the Sun, never straying too far from it and only revealing itself within a few hours of sunrise or sunset. Venus has two distinctly different lives or manifestations; as a *morning star* it rises before the Sun in the east, and as an *evening star* it sets with the Sun in the west. In between these morning and evening appearances, Venus is invisible; it disappears into the Sun. In its evening star phase, Mesoamerican skywatchers saw Venus as the one who pushes the Sun down into the underworld. The Aztec deity Xolotl, a dog-like god of the underworld, was associated with Venus in this phase. After disappearing behind the Sun for a few days, Venus is reborn as a morning star and leads the Sun into the sky. At this point in its cycle Venus was considered militant and dangerous and was said to strike at the Earth. It was this morning star phase, considered the most important of the two at least for calculation purposes, in which

Venus was personified by Quetzalcoatl, first priest, bringer of culture, and the god who sinned.[2] In order to better understand this association of the planet Venus with this very important mythologized man-god, we will first examine the astronomy of the planet Venus and the manner in which the Maya reckoned its positions in space and time, and then consider the mysterious figure of Quetzalcoatl in his various manifestations.

The Cycle of Venus

Although the planet Venus orbits the Sun in 225 days, called its sidereal period, it is not this motion that is apparent to an earthbound observer. What is seen from the vantage point of the earth is a cycle of phases that repeat on the average every 584 days.[3] This cycle is called its synodic period; its cycle of relationship with the Sun. Suppose we start this cycle as the Mesoamerican astronomers did, with the heliacal rising (the first day that Venus becomes visible in its morning star phase). The heliacal rising occurs when Venus is separated from the Sun by about 6 to 10 degrees, just a few days (traditionally four) after the planet's conjunction with the Sun.[4] In an astronomical ephemeris, this event occurs when Venus is retrograde. This conjunction is called an *inferior* conjunction because Venus is located between the Sun and the Earth; Venus, the inferior body, stands in front of the Sun, the superior body. On this first day of the Venus cycle, the observer would see Venus appear a few degrees above the horizon in the twilight for only a few minutes. Its light would soon be extinguished by the more powerful light of the rising Sun which is brought closer to the horizon by the rotating earth. On the next day, Venus is at a greater distance from the Sun because it is moving retrograde while the Sun is moving ahead in the zodiac, and the morning star shines for a longer period and appears much brighter. Within a few days, Venus reaches its greatest brilliance because of its elongation from the Sun and its proximity to the Earth in this phase.

The Maya thought Venus at its heliacal rising to be dangerous and an unlucky omen. In fact, some of their names for Venus translate as "wasp star" or "spearing god," and the day-sign or trecena on which the heliacal rising occurred was considered to be an indicator of its specific power and action at that time. This was an event that was generally feared by the populace and even a direct gaze at the planet was considered extremely dangerous. Friar Sahagún in his history of New Spain writes:

"Of the morning star, the great star, it was said that when it first emerged and came forth, four times it vanished and disappeared quickly. And afterwards it burst forth completely, took its place in full light, became brilliant, and shone white. Like the moon's rays, so did it shine. And when it newly emerged, much fear came over them; all were frightened. Everywhere the outlets and openings [of houses] were closed up. It was said that perchance [the light] might bring a cause of sickness, something evil, when it came to emerge. But sometimes it was regarded as benevolent."[5]

The 584-day Venus cycle contains 29 cycles of the 20 day-signs with 4 days left over. Because of this, and assuming the Venus cycle is a constant 584 days, the heliacal rising of Venus would occur on only 5 of the day-signs. In Maya times these were Ahau, Kan, Lamat, Eb and Cib, all five being day-signs of the south direction. This relationship of cycles allows for a rough accounting of the Venus cycle as the never-ending, non-adjusting 260-day astrological calendar rolled along.

Venus remains a morning star for about 263 days on average, first increasing its zodiacal distance from the Sun and reaching greatest elongation (47 degrees from the Sun), and then closing in on it again. At this point Venus moves toward *superior* conjunction with the Sun and its greatest astronomical distance from the Earth. The planet now becomes invisible, because of its proximity to the Sun, for about 50 days. In an astronomical ephemeris this is shown as Venus and the Sun moving together in conjunction at roughly the same speed. After this disappearance interval, Venus makes its appearance as an evening star and remains in that phase for another 263 days on average. As Venus moves closer to the Sun in the zodiac and heads toward inferior conjunction, it becomes more brilliant. Finally, Venus disappears in the Sun's rays for only a few days and then makes a dramatic reappearance as a bright morning star. The 584-day cycle thus begins again -- but this time at a different point in the zodiac and on a different day-sign.

During a period of 8 years, Venus will complete five synodic cycles. Using a rounded off figure of 365 days for the solar year and 584 for the Venus year we arrive at an interesting match. 8 x 365 is the same as 5 x 584. Using exact figures for solar year (365.2422 x 8 = 2,921.9376) and Venus year (583.92 x 5 = 2,919.6), we have a discrepancy of about 2.3 days between the two -- still a remarkably close match.[6] Even more remarkable is the fact that every 6th Venus cycle occurs in the same part of the sky. The five Venus cycles in an 8-year period occur in sections of the zodiac that are about 72 degrees (1/5 of a circle, or a quintile) apart from each other. For example, the Venus/Sun inferior conjunction of 11/2/1994 occurs at 10 degrees of Scorpio (tropical zodiac). Eight years prior, on 11/5/1986, a Venus/Sun inferior conjunction occurred at 12 degrees of Scorpio. Over an 8-year period, then, the spatial position of the Venus/Sun inferior conjunction moves backwards in the zodiac by about 2.34 degrees. At this rate, a complete cycle of these inferior conjunctions around the zodiac (770 Venus years of 584 days) takes about 1231 solar years.[7]

Besides the phase changes and the 8-year spatial shift of the planet Venus, its rising and setting positions against the horizon were of interest to Mesoamerican astronomers. A full rising or setting cycle also takes eight solar years, or five Venus periods of 584 days to complete. Once every eight years Venus reaches its extreme northerly or southerly rising or setting positions. To track this pattern, certain Maya temples and observatories were specifically aligned to horizon features or had special windows or sighting tubes designed to locate a particular rising or setting position.

There are two well-known examples of ancient architectural con-structs that contain alignments to the extreme horizon positions of Venus in Yucatan, Mexico.[8] Uxmal is a late classic ceremonial center located near Merida and is in the vicinity of several other large centers built at the same time. At Uxmal is a large building known as the Governor's Palace, a long building with extensive frieze work over a series of entrances to various inner chambers. The center opening is square and somewhat larger than the others flanking it. Standing in this doorway, one can look out to an unobstructed horizon. On the horizon, directly in front of the door and appearing as a small speck in the distance, can be seen the remains of the principal pyramid of Nohpat, one of the other nearby ceremonial centers. From the central doorway of the Governor's Palace, Venus would have set (around 800 AD) directly over this distant pyramid at its maximum southerly horizon position which occurs every 8 years. The Governor's Palace could therefore have been used as Venus observatory.

At Chichen Itza, a complex site northeast of Uxmal, is found the famous Caracol, the best surviving example of a Maya round tower. Round temples in Mesoamerica were usually associated with Quetzalcoatl/Venus in his manifestation as the wind god. The Caracol (meaning snail in Maya, a reference to the spiral inner staircase of this building) appears to have been built, at least in part, for the purpose of noting rising and setting positions of astronomical bodies, including Venus. From the upper level, at least two of the surviving three windows could have been used to locate the extreme setting positions of Venus and hence to time the entire cycle. The skywatcher in the temple of Figure 3 is shown looking through crossed sticks, a observational astronomy technique that was probably used in the windows of the Caracol.

The Maya divided the cycle of Venus into 4 sections and assigned them figures that differ from those that are astronomically correct. In the Dresden Codex, the picture and number script gives dates of the various intervals of the Venus synodic cycle for a period of 5 Venus cycles or 8 solar years. These dates are also tied into the calendar round and include divinatory information. In these tables, however, the length of morning and evening phase, and also the length of superior conjunction, differ from the astronomically correct figures. The only interval that is accurately represented is the interval of inferior conjunction, which is 8 days; the other intervals are distorted. This ritualistic scheme of Venus phenomena, as laid out in the Dresden Codex, is as follows:

1. Visibility as morning star - 236 days (actual 263)

2. Invisibility at superior conjunction - 90 days (actual 50)
3. Visibility as evening star - 250 days (actual 263)
4. Invisibility at inferior conjunction - 8 days

Apparently, Maya astronomers were willing to alter the short term Venus intervals in favor of linking them with other astronomical and ritual cycles. It is possible that linkage with the lunation cycle is an explanation, because 236 days is equal to 8 lunations and 250 days equals 8 1/2 lunations. This would allow an observer to time Venus cycle changes by referring to a specific phase of the Moon.[9] Surviving tables, including those in the Dresden (Figure 9) and Grolier Codices, predict the beginning dates for each of the ritualistic Venus intervals and also give an astrological interpretation for each. The interpretations are based on correlations with the 260-day calendar.

Except for these distorted figures, the almanac is extremely accurate. A brief account of the contents of the Dresden Codex will illustrate the use and accuracy of these tables for Venus phenomena. First, the Codex is essentially a table of Venus interval positions for a period of 8 solar years or five Venus cycles. The tables seem to have been designed to be used over long periods of time and appear to have built-in corrections for the errors that accumulate due to short term astronomical fluctuations. For example, if one were to follow the tables for two calendar rounds (104 years), a period they were apparently designed for, a slippage of 5 days would occur between the heliacal rising of Venus and that predicted in the tables. In addition, the 584-day count is an average; in a given year the predicted phenomena could be up to several days off. Thompson suggested that such corrections could be made if the user of the tables would stop at specific points, subtract a specified number of days, and then return to the beginning of the table. This approach would keep the tables accurate to within 2 hours over 481 years.[10]

The Venus calendar of the Dresden Codex (one page is shown in Figure 9) consists of both astronomical data and accompanying astrological omens. The omens are all bad ones, pointing to crop disasters, disease, and other troubles. These omens are each connected with the five times in 8 years that Venus makes its heliacal

Figure 9. A page from the Venus tables of the Dresden Codex. The middle picture shows Venus spearing the victim, a frog-god, below. The glyphs and numbers link the Venus cycle with the calendar.

rise and "spears" victims on earth. There are five depictions of this spearing Venus, one for each 584-day cycle. The victims are (in order) an old god, a jaguar, the maize god, a frog god, and a youth.

Some more specific astrological interpretations of the particular effects of the heliacal rising of Venus have survived in post- Conquest writings. Besides the Dresden Codex, a written account of the effects of the heliacal rising is also found in the Anales de Quauhtitlan, a colonial document from Mexico, translated below. According to this source, the 13-day period in which the rising occurred indicated exactly who or what would be struck by the spearing Venus.

"If the helical rising fell 1-Crocodile and 1-Ocelot, Venus shot at old men and women equally. When in 1-Ocelot, 1-Deer, and 1- Flower, it shot the little children. If in 1-Reed or 1-Death, it shot important lords. If in 1-Rain it shot the rain so it would not rain. If in 1-Movement, it shot youths and maidens, and in 1- Water all was dry." [11]

It is an interesting coincidence that the 584-day cycle (or year) of Venus links with the solar year; 5 Venus years equaling 8 solar years. Because of this relationship, the Venus year dovetails with the 260-day count and the 52-year calendar round; sixty five 584-day Venus years is exactly equal to 104 solar years or 146 repeats of the 260-day divinatory cycle. Notice that this figure also equals 2 calendar rounds of 52 solar years each. It is this kind of pattern perception that allowed the Maya to arrive at such exact measurements of the various astronomical cycles. They did not rely on fractions to define periods, they merely linked one cycle with another, even if huge numbers were involved. This approach in no way hindered their accuracy; in fact, it gave them tremendous numerical control over their celestial environment. Besides knowing just when an astronomical event would occur, they knew how it related to other events.

Seler suggested that it was this peculiar Sun/Venus relationship which led to the original creation of the 260-day period and the tonalamatl arrangement of twenty 13-day periods. [12] He argues that in the 8-year period when Venus has five periods of 584 days, the total number of days, 2,920 (365 x 8) can be expressed as 5 x 8 x 73. Now 73 is the number that when multiplied by five equals one solar year, and when multiplied by eight equals one Venus year. One solar year of 365 days plus one Venus year of 584 days equals 949 days, and this also is equal to 13 x 73. Seler takes the 949-day figure (the sum of a solar year and a Venus year) as a basic unit, which incredibly turns out to be 1/20th of a 52 year cycle, the so-called Mesoamerican century or calendar round. So then 20 x 949 = 18,980 days or 52 years. If each of these 949-day periods are divided by 73, thirteen periods of 73 days results. In one 52-year cycle there are, therefore, 260 periods of 73 days. 73 days, exactly 1/5 of a solar year, is then like one day-sign in a 52-year calendar round. Another interesting twist to this exercise in numerical relationships is that 260 divided by five equals 52. In Seler's argument, these mind-boggling numerological gymnastics are the secret behind the origin of the 260-day astrological calendar. Seler also suggested that because only five of the twenty named days can fall on the first day of a Venus cycle, the Mesoamerican astrologers arranged the tonalamatl in vertical columns of five signs each. However complicated this argument sounds, it does show subtle, but impressive, linkages between the Sun, Venus, the 52-year cycle and the tonalamatl.

Quetzalcoatl

Having explored the astronomical dynamics of the planet Venus and described some of the methods employed in tracking and analyzing its cycle, we now turn to myth. Perhaps the best known god of ancient Mexico was Quetzalcoatl who was always linked to or identified with the planet Venus. The name Quetzalcoatl is a composite of quetzal, a beautiful, plumed bird of the central American jungles, and coatl which means serpent. Another interpretation of this name is "Precious Twin," a reference to the dual appearances of the planet Venus. A third name is Ce Acatl, or 1-Reed, the day-sign of Quetzalcoatl. Finally, the Maya name for this god was Kukulcan.

In the older pre-Columbian codices, Quetzalcoatl was a culture hero, called 9-Wind, who ascended to the heavens and returned to earth to create cosmic and terrestrial space.[13] In the codices (and on this book's cover illustration) he is shown descending from the heavens carrying symbols of the planet Venus, flanked by the Sun and Moon. Arriving on earth, he separates the sky from the primordial waters. Later sources on Quetzalcoatl are somewhat contradictory; sometimes he is a god, sometimes a man and founder of a royal lineage. The common theme in these later stories concerns the flowering of the Toltec empire (Postclassic) and its destruction. During Toltec times at least one leader, usually referred to as Topiltzin-Quetzalcoatl, took the name Quetzalcoatl for himself. The name also appears to have been a title for an esoteric priesthood. In these stories Quetzalcoatl is associated with right conduct as a leader, the correct performance of ritual, a happy, healthy economy, and personal sacrifice. The myth tells of black magicians introducing Quetzalcoatl to pulque, an intoxicating beverage, so that he falls from grace and witnesses the destruction of culture.

Much has been written on this fascinating and mysterious god or culture hero. Carrasco (1982), in a lengthy analysis of the various surviving records, suggests that Quetzalcoatl was in essence a widespread cultural symbol of civilization itself, the priesthood, and the triumph of order over chaos. The ceremonial center, the visible symbol of Mesoamerican integrity, is suggested by Carrasco to be linked to Quetzalcoatl. But as a symbol, the formality of the ceremonial center (the social world in complete and perfect form) also includes the suggestion of eventual destruction. In this view, man's conquest over chaos is temporary. Within stability lie the seeds of destruction. This notion can be seen in the various versions of the Toltec Topilzin-Quetzalcoatl myth.

In the Toltec myth, found in the Anales De Cuauhtitlan[14], Quetzalcoatl was a man of high birth whose father had died before he was born. He made his way up in society as a priest and eventually reached the highest position possible, that of Toltec chief and high priest. He established his own style of religion and followed his spiritual practices impeccably, forbidding the sacrifice of anything but snakes and butterflies. Over time, Quetzalcoatl became obsessed with doing his penances and other rituals and sequestered himself behind his temple walls. Meanwhile, his sorcerer enemies, including the dark god Tezcatlipoca who later became one of the primary gods of the Aztecs, plotted to bring him down and introduce human sacrifice. Tezcatlipoca got past the temple guards and presented Quetzalcoatl with a mirror in which he saw himself -- and how ugly he had become. One of the other sorcerers offered to dress Quetzalcoatl up in the best feathers and then he introduced him to the intoxicating beverage pulque. After five cups of the brew, and in a state of drunkenness, Quetzalcoatl broke his vows of chastity and had sex with his sister. The shame of this act caused him to abandon his throne and begin a long march towards the east. On his way he made some important stops, paid homage to the various gods and eventually arrived at the shoreline. There he set himself on fire from which many beautiful and valuable birds arose. His heart was the quetzal bird itself which entered the sky and became the planet Venus. The story goes on to say that when Quetzalcoatl died, he went to Mictlan (the underworld) for 4 days and then in another 4 days appeared as Venus in the east, armed with arrows and spears. Quetzalcoatl's life began in the year 1- Reed and ended 52 years later, also in 1-Reed.

Friar Sahagún recounts another version of this Topilzin-Quetzalcoatl story.[15] It begins with Quetzalcoatl in his prime, revered as the god-king of Tula, the capital city of the Toltecs. Everything was perfect, abundant and beautiful in the kingdom. Eventually, though, the people of Tula became slothful and opened themselves to being tricked by the same three dark sorcerers of the Anales De Cuauhtitlan version. Inciting anxiety and confusion by exploiting sexual desires, using pulque to wear down self-control, and creating chaos by performing strange tricks, the three succeeded in humiliating Quetzalcoatl and causing him to abandon the city. He then wandered through various places leaving an imprint of one sort or another until reaching the sea where he built a raft of serpents and sailed away into the east.

Among the Maya, the cult of the feathered serpent appears to be very old, and a number of sculptures depicting this figure are to be found among the ruined temples. But not much else is known about the myth from these parts of Mesoamerica, with the exception of a few references in the Popol Vuh, which will be mentioned later in this chapter. In Yucatan there is also the story of Kukulcan, a Toltec chief, who reorganized the decaying Maya cities and rebuilt Chichen

Itza, bringing it to its greatest glory. He is also said to have introduced human sacrifice, graphically illustrated by the sculptures throughout the site. This part of the story is obviously inconsistent with the rest of the Quetzalcoatl legend.

The mythology of Quezalcoatl is confusing and uncertain, but for our purposes a few conclusions can be drawn. First, Quetzalcoatl seems to have always been associated with the planet Venus, particularly in its morning star phase. Secondly, he was either a god who brought culture and civilization, a traditional priesthood, or a leader who self-sacrificed so as to maintain the proper rituals on which social stability depended. Eventually he failed, self-destructed and was born again. Quetzalcoatl was therefore associated with ceremonial centers and temples, the physical embodiments of civilized man's attempts to recreate the order of the universe. Third, he was associated with the air and with winds, evidenced by the many round temples dedicated to his manifestation as Ehecatl, the bearded, snout-nosed wind god. Finally, the Quetzalcoatl myth illustrates an archetypal spiritual path, including its pitfalls. He is the man who strives for perfection but falls from grace through loss of control of his passions because he fails to recognize his dark side. He eventually sacrifices himself and returns as a particularly masculine morning star. He is creative, an artist, a ritual and calendar expert, an astrologer, a civilizer, prophet, priest, and martyr all in one. The power of this myth was such that the leaders of the Aztec empire, the mightiest political center in all of Mexico at the time of Cortés' arrival, were probably weakened psychologically by the suspicion that the bearded Cortés, who arrived in the year 1-Reed, was the returning Quetzalcoatl.

There was in Mesoamerican myth a darker counterpart to Quetzalcoatl call Xolotl. He was an ancient god known as "the animal," the one who pushed the Sun back into darkness, and was associated with Venus in its evening star phase. Xolotl was a deformed creature, with a dog-like head, repellent, lame, and considered a bringer of bad luck. On the other hand, Xolotl was also known as the bringer of both fire from the underworld, his natural realm. While it seems apparent that the ancient Mesoamericans knew that Venus in both its phases was but one planet, they also made a strong distinction between its qualities when in one phase or the other. As an evening star, Venus heralds the onset of the night, the dark, and the rule of the underworld. Quetzalcoatl and Xolotl were thus two manifestations of the same planet, two ways of expressing what the Mesoamericans believed or found to be true about this bright object in the sky. The meaning of the two phases of Venus seems to have been incorporated into the ritual athletic life of the culture itself, as we will now see.

The Ball Game

The ancient Mesoamerican peoples appear to have made efforts to pattern ritual aspects of their cultural life after the movements of the planet Venus in a ritualistic ball game. There is evidence that ritual observances, such as coronations, were tailored to correspond to this visible cycle, and that some dates of certain historical events were even changed to fit the pattern. Some of the most dramatic evidence we have of this culturally recreated astronomical drama is with the ball game itself.

The ball game, called Tlachtli by the Aztecs, was played throughout ancient Mesoamerica from very early times, even as early as -900 by the Olmecs. It is not clear today exactly how the game was played, but we know there were two teams who played against each other in a specially constructed court. They moved a hard rubber ball around, soccer style, using their hips, legs and buttocks, but not their hands. The players wore heavy padding of cotton and leather to protect themselves from what was, apparently, a very rough game. In some courts, a large ring or hoop was suspended on each side of mid court. Presumably, a ball shot through one of these rings would win the game.

The ball game figures prominently in the Maya story of the Hero Twins told in the Popol Vuh, the book of council or Maya bible. In this creation epic the conflict between the upper world and underworld (Xibalba/Mictlan), the conflict of life and death, of health and disease, is played out by the Hero Twins in ball games with the Lords of Xibalba. Avenging their father's death in an earlier game with the Lords, the Hero Twins Hunahpu and Xbalanque defeat the

Lords of Xibalba through cunning, tricks and a willingness to sacrifice themselves and lose in the short term in order to win the final victory.

There are some intriguing correlations in the Popol Vuh myth in regard to the Venus cycle. To begin with, the names of the Hero Twins and their fathers, 1-Hunahpu and 7-Hunahpu, are suggestive of Venus and the Sun. Hunahpu is the Quiche Maya name for Hun-Ahau, or 1-Ahau, the day-sign of the first of the five Venus cycles listed in the Dresden Codex. This day-sign comes up at the top of a Venus cycle only once every 8 years. Also, the Hero Twins themselves pass through a series of what are probably five test houses in the underworld. They are described early in the myth as the Dark House, the Rattling House, the Jaguar House, the Bat House, and the House of Knives.[16] These may correlate with the five Venus stations over 8 years. It has also been suggested that Hunahpu and Xbalanque were themselves Venus and the Sun, not the Moon and Sun as the text suggests at the end of the tale.

At the archeological site of El Tajin, a late-Classic Gulf Coast center northeast of the valley of Mexico, is a ball court containing a number of panels that have been interpreted as describing the ceremonial playing of the ball game coincident with several astronomical cycles, particularly the Venus cycle. Cook de Leonard (1975) has suggested that ceremonial events leading up to the game were determined by a time frame created by the movement of Venus. De Lenard notes that the lunar phases in the panels are consistent with the four ritual divisions of the Venus cycle in the Dresden Codex and may have been crucial in denoting the exact date of each happening.

The first panel at El Tajin correlates with Venus as an evening star and appears to show a candidate (ball player) taking vows of purity. According to legend this is the part of the Venus cycle when Venus takes the form of a man and walks the earth. This corresponds with Quetzalcoatl wandering the earth as he heads to the sea before self-destruction and rebirth as the morning star. In the next panel, which corresponds to Venus as a morning star, the candidate spends the night with music, drink and love; influenced by the god of lust and love he loses control and commits sins. There appears to be a product of this sin, the birth of a sky monster. In the third panel, disappearance behind the Sun (superior conjunction) the ball game is played in the underworld. Venus has lost the game and accepts sacrifice by the Sun. In the fourth panel, which covers the span from evening star, inferior conjunction and on to morning star, Venus is sacrificed. The death of Venus occurs while the planet is obscured by the Sun during inferior conjunction, but ultimately Venus is reborn as a morning star. Cook de Leonard suggests that, because the phase of the Moon is shown in the various panels depicting the cycle of Venus, it may be the Moon that is used as a day timer and hence is the source of the astronomically inaccurate tabulation of 236 and 250 days for periods that are actually 263 days.

Venus-Regulated Warfare

In several of the ancient codices, Venus is portrayed as a male warrior who is shooting or spearing a victim. As we have already seen, five such poses accompany the Venus cycle data in the Dresden Codex and are regarded by interpreters as omens; they were forecasts or predictions for each of the five Venus appearance dates. The Aztec Venus god was Tlahuizcalpantecuhtli, or "Dawn House Lord," a definitely militant and masculine figure. Clearly, the Mesoamericans did not regard Venus as female and certainly, with the exception of the softer side of Quetzalcoatl and the connections with social stability, they did not connect this planet with peace. Quite on the contrary, recent research has shown that a large number of battle dates, recorded in stone, coincide with Venus phenomena, especially first appearances as evening star, morning star, or some other significant point in its cycle such as greatest elongation. That these recorded dates are so closely tied to Venus phenomena strongly suggests that warfare must have been at times ritualistic and quite possibly planned around the movements of this planet.[17]

As the dynastic histories encoded on stone of the various Maya kingdoms were decoded over the past three decades, it became apparent that the source of ritual Venus-regulated warfare was from the greatest of Classic centers, Teotihuacan in the Mexican highlands. The inscriptions, murals, and painted pottery revealed that it was a new style of warfare, one that used different weaponry and different costuming, as well as synchronization with critical junctures in the Venus cycle and other planet stationary points. This military style has come to be called Tlaloc-Venus Warfare, Tlaloc being a rain/war god of the Teotihuacanos whose attributes are found in the archaeological record. Connections between the five Venus cycles in 8 years and sacrificial enclosures have been made by researchers who now look on Venus tables such as those in the Dresden Codex as being 8-year Venus war almanacs.[18]

In the astrology of ancient Mesoamerica the planet Venus was used as a timer of ceremonial, athletic, and militaristic events. It was also used for forecasting and played a major part in the astronomical divinatory system associated with the 260-day calendar. Venus' motions were bent to match more exactly the short term phenomena, notably the lunations, but there was confidence in the overall pattern because of the precise linkage of the much larger cycles. Most striking, and an example of a rudimentary type of "planetary astrology," is the emphasis on the power of Venus when it was at heliacal rising. Also, distinctions between each of the five Venus cycles in any given 8-year period were made in Mesoamerica. All this suggests there are new ways for modern astrologers to interpret the influence of the planet Venus. These notions will be expanded upon in the last chapter.

Chapter 7

Maya Time Constructs and The Long Count

As we have seen, the ancient Mesoamericans astrologers built their astrological system on the changing patterns of light and dark created by the rotation of the earth. The Sun's creation of the alternation of light and dark was their model of both order and continuity, and change and renewal. The Maya, who developed the most sophisticated astronomical and astrological systems in Mesoamerica, used the term "kin" in reference to the Sun, to the day and to time itself. All three were seen to be intimately interconnected. Sun, day and time were three aspects of one concept.

In previous chapters we have seen how each individual day was a sign in itself and had a specific meaning. Days were also grouped together to form units of time that had specific meanings, i.e. the 9, 13 and 20-day periods. In effect, time itself became symbolic of life, and as such became the principal component of the astrological-divinatory system that evolved in Mesoamerica. In Mesoamerican astrology, blocks of time operate much like spatial zodiac signs do in Western astrology.

Before delving into the complexities of Maya calendrics, it may be appropriate to briefly comment on the numerology that lies behind the multitude of cycles we are about to explore. Throughout the entire Mesoamerican culture area certain numbers assumed importance over others. These were duplicated frequently in the length of cycles, the groupings of the various gods, in artistic designs and even in the structure of the community itself. Four was the number of the Sun because its yearly motions defined the four directions (see Figure 1). Five was important because it was the center, or apex of the four directions. Four and five combine in architecture as the pyramid (four sides plus the apex), and when added together equal nine, regarded as a powerful and dark number. Most mysterious is the special emphasis on the number thirteen which is found in nearly every important cycle in some way or another. Why thirteen rather than twelve? It is possible that this number was originally suggested from the thirteen lunations in a given year, but other cultures settled on twelve which is a more "workable" number, being divisible by 2, 3, 4 and 6. Of course, thirteen is twelve with a center or apex. Twenty was also important and probably has its origins in the digits of the human body. These last two numbers in combination, thirteen and twenty, established the basic numerological framework of ancient Mesoamerica. In combination they form the 260- day calendar and other important time-periods which will now be introduced.

The Long Count

During the Classic Period, the Maya developed Mesoamerica's most elaborate time-keeping tradition. Sequences of days were counted, associated with specific deities, and given symbolic meanings. Numerous cycles meshed with each other, joining at key moments as if to re-affirm an underlying common denominator. For the Maya, life was an ongoing succession of individual time periods each of which had a predictable quality. Knowledge of time was at the basis of their astrology, theology, cosmology, and history. For them, the purpose of life was to conform to the sky rhythms that had created time and to reflect in daily life and in their civilization the orderliness of cyclic repetitions. Below is a listing of the major time cycles used by the Maya of the Classic Period.

Cycles of the Maya

1 day = 1 kin
20 kins = 1 uinal (20 days)
18 uinals = 1 tun (360 days)
20 tuns = 1 katun (7,200 days or 19.71 years)
13 katuns = 1 katun cycle (93,600 days or 256.27 years)
20 katuns = 1 baktun (144,000 days or 394.26 years)
13 baktuns = 1 creation epoch (5125.37 years)

For the Maya the day, or kin, was the most basic unit of time. One of the glyphs used to represent this unit was a four petaled flower. The flower, representing procreation, and the number four, were both symbols of the Sun. Additionally, the symbol for kin was that of the Sun god himself. A period of 20 days, the "uinal" (which comes from the root word for man), was the next basic time unit.

The "tun" was next, a unit of 360 days and just short of a solar year. As the Maya were concerned with ordering enormous periods of symbolic time, they undoubtedly found the number 360 much easier to work with than 365.24, the actual length of the solar year. The tun is not to be confused with the haab or 365-day year.[1] Tun means stone or "precious stone" and seems to refer to jade or other green stones in particular. The Maya frequently erected stone monuments at the end or beginning of a time period. The close approximation of the tun with the solar year suggests its importance as a "milestone" of sorts. There are also some linguistic connections with water, or precious water, for the tun.

A cycle of 20 tuns is a "katun," a term that is probably a shortening of kal-tun, kal meaning 20. The length of a katun is 20 x 360 or 7,200 days. The katun was perhaps the most celebrated time unit for the Maya. Many stone monuments, called stelae, are found throughout the culture region commemorating historical events, dynasty transitions, wars, and the passage from one katun to another. An example of what might be called time-period mundane astrology is shown by the Maya cycle of thirteen katuns, first documented by Bishop Landa during the mid 16th century.[2] In this time period, thirteen katuns of 7,200 days completed a full katun cycle. Each individual katun had its own name and associated deity, and also its own type of worship, rites, and sacrifices. According to Landa, the patron deity ruling each katun was worshiped exclusively for the first ten years of his rule. The second half of the katun was shared with his successor, who would then become an object of respect. In other words, the process of rulership change began at the midpoint of the cycle, although full rulership change occurred upon completion. Each of the twenty tuns that made up a katun had a specific prophecy as well.

The Cycle of the 13 Katuns

The 256-year cycle of thirteen katuns, a post-classic chronological system, has come to be known to students of Mayan calendrics as the "short count". The manner of distinguishing the katuns from each other involves the day-signs and the inherent precision of the system itself. The name of each katun in the cycle is taken from the day on which the period ends, or reaches completion. Each of the thirteen katuns in the cycle is indicated by a number and the name Ahau, this being the day of the 260-day calendar on which the last day of the katun falls. The first day, therefore, of any given katun always falls on the day Imix, which follows Ahau and is usually considered to be the first of the twenty named days. Because 20 is one factor of the katun cycle (20 x 360), each katun always ends on a day with the same name in the 260-day calendar, though not on the same number.

The katuns did not follow each other in numerical order. Any given katun in the cycle was always followed by a katun that was numbered two less. For example, katun 10-Ahau was followed by Katun 8-Ahau. This can be seen more clearly on the "katun wheel" (Figure 10) which should be read in a clockwise direction. The katun from which the cycle began was katun 11-Ahau. The reason for this was that the previous katun ended with the last day in the 260-day calendar, the day 13-Ahau, which gives its name to that katun. The very next day is the 1-Imix, the first day of the 260-day calendar, and it begins katun 11-Ahau. The katun wheel in Figure 10, drawn by Landa, shows the order of the katun cycle. The cross over katun 11-Ahau indicates the starting point of the cycle. The thirteen face glyphs are for the day Ahau; the numbers are in both Roman numerals and in the Maya language. In the Books of Chilam Balam are found similar katun wheels and diagrams showing the thirteen Lords of the katuns, although, unfortunately, these Lords are drawn to look like Spanish kings, not like the original gods who ruled the katuns.[3]

There are interesting correlations of planetary cycles with these important Maya time periods. A katun of 7,200 days is 19.71 years, very close to the Jupiter-Saturn cycle of 19.86 years. The complete cycle of 13 katuns is 256.26 years, close to double the Uranus-Pluto cycle which is 254.98 years. It would seem that over time, the two katuns of the 13 katun cycle which contained Uranus-Pluto conjunctions would stand out as times of social change, and because the timing is so close, the coincidence would be constant over a long period of time. It is certainly interesting that in regard to the listing of katuns above, the Uranus- Pluto conjunctions during that period occur in 1201 and 1456, both in katun 8-Ahau, regarded as a katun of major crises and changes. According to Maya history, the major center Chichen Itza was conquered in 1201 and the destruction of Mayapan, the last of the Mayan centers in Yucatan, occurred in 1458. The single katun itself, being so close to the Jupiter/Saturn cycle, was probably an excellent time keeper and monitor for socio-political developments. The point I am making is that by adhering to a calendar that reproduces outstanding natural cycles, the Maya were able to understand and regulate their history and future. Maya cycles were exacting abstractions from nature, pure mathematical biorhythms.[4]

Essentially, the cycle of thirteen katuns was for the Maya a kind of mundane astrology, not an astrology of the individual, but of the society and its history. Each katun had its own particular fate that allowed for prophecy. In the several books of Chilam Balam, the influences of the thirteen katuns are stated, usually as a description of historical events that occurred during each katun. It becomes clear to the reader, however, that the Maya always expected history to repeat itself, and that the katuns had their own individual fates. It is also obvious that the Maya were not very optimistic about their fate since most of these "fates" are negative, but then this may have been was how life was for them. The delineations below are a composite taken from the Book of Chilam Balam of Chumayel and the Codex Perez and the Book of Chilam Balam of Mani.

11-Ahau: Death from starvation. Great weeping and invading foreigners. Scant rains.

9-Ahau: Rulers share power with priests. Many diseases, wars and much adultery.

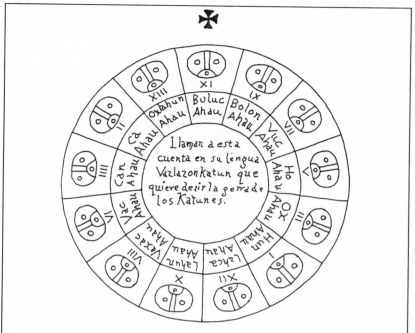

The katun wheel from Landa. The clockwise sequence of katuns begins at the top with katun 11-Ahau, followed by katun 9-Ahau, katun 7-Ahau etc.

7-Ahau: Lust, carnal sin, and excesses.

5-Ahau: Harshness. The people lose faith in their rulers. There are few births.

3-Ahau: Misfortunes and calamities. Envy ends and wisdom comes to the unfortunate.

1-Ahau: Filth and shame in government. Rivalries. A great war.

12-Ahau: Government and obedience. Abundance. The poor become rich. There is still some destruction.

10-Ahau: Famine. Discord between foreign governors and their subjects. Drought.

8-Ahau: Demolition and destruction. Conflicts among leaders. The end of governments.

6-Ahau: Deception, starvation and ruin. Rulers have difficulty governing.

4-Ahau: Food scarcities. Half the katun good, half bad. The return of Kukulkan.

2-Ahau: For half the katun there will be bread, for half water. The end of the word of God.

13-Ahau: Famine, plagues of locusts, and loss of rulers. The judgment of God.

During the course of a typical lifetime, an individual might witness the passage of two or more katuns. The Maya, however, did not limit their sense of time-keeping to just a lifetime, they took on numbers that stagger the imagination. The next time unit after the katun is the "baktun", a unit composed of 20 katuns or 400 tuns, about 394 solar years. A cycle of 13 baktuns, 5,125 years, is a creation epoch and the basis of the Long Count discussed below. Extending beyond this span was the "pictun," which is 20 baktuns or 8,000 tuns, and the "calabtun" of 20 pictuns or 160,000 tuns. The next order is the "kinchiltun" of 20 calabtuns and possibly not finally, the "alautun" of 20 kinchiltuns. This last time unit, the alautun is about 63 million years in length, quite a stretch for a culture that only flourished for about a thousand years.

With the exception of the tun, which is derived from 18 uinals, all the time periods mentioned above are made up of 20 of the previous unit. It appears then that 13 units of a time period have a specialized and astrological/divinatory meaning. For example, 13 uinals of 20 days equals 260 days, the length of the 260-day count. Thirteen katuns of twenty tuns (260 tuns) equals one katun cycle (short count) as described by Landa. As we have already seen, each katun was said to have a particular meaning and was assigned specific gods as rulers. Beyond the cycle of katuns is the cycle of 13 baktuns which is the Long Count or a creation epoch.

The creation epoch of 13 baktuns in length has a specific starting and ending point in time. Although there are some differences of opinion, most scholars agree that the beginning of the present creation epoch, or cycle of 13 baktuns, began on or about August 11, -3113.[5] The Maya dated their stelae and other monuments, as well as their history, from this date. The Maya inscriptions designate any particular date by noting the number of the baktuns, katuns, tuns, uinals, and kins which have elapsed since the beginning of the present creation epoch. This measurement from the zero date is called the Long Count.[6]

The correlation of the Mayan calendar with the European calendars is based on a few dates recorded in documents around the time of the Conquest in both calendars and also inscriptions of dates on stone that can be linked with known astronomical events. For archaeologists and astronomers, the correlation problem is complicated by the fact that inscriptions and manuscripts contain both calendar dates and astronomical data. As a result, various correlations have been proposed and argued, and until recently, the matter was far from settled. At the present time, the Goodman-Martinez-Thompson correlation has withstood much testing and has become the most widely accepted. A further discussion of this correlation problem will be found in Chapter 9.

The cycle of 13 baktuns, which forms the Long Count/creation epoch, is of special interest to our study. To begin with, the length of the unit, 5,125 years, is very close to 1/5 of a precessional cycle. The precessional cycle, or precession of the equinoxes, is the movement of the vernal point (intersection of Earth's projected equator and Earth's orbit around the Sun) against the fixed stars. One circuit through the stars of the equinox takes approximately 25,695 years. One fifth of this figure is 5139 years -- just 15 years larger than the creation epoch, an extremely small error considering the length of time involved.[7] Before discussing the various creation myths, it should be pointed out that such a division of the precessional cycle is not unknown in Western astrology. The so-called "ages" (ie. age of Aquarius) in Western astrology result from a division of this cycle by the number 12.   We have here a case of the same astronomical cycle   computed, divided, and interpreted by both Western and Mesoamerican astrologers.

We know that the 260-day astrological calendar lies at the heart of Mesoamerican astrology. Each day has its own specific meaning or "fate" and its place in the order. The "short count," or cycle of 13 katuns, contains 260 tuns and the Long Count itself contains 260 katuns.   These units of time are actually macro versions of the divinatory calendar, segments of time that are divided into 260 symbolic "days."   The Maya believed that similar components of sacred time units, for example the first day of the tzolkin or the first tun of the short count, had shared characteristics. They recognized a kind of parallel resonance between these blocks of time that was used for forecasting and planning. What we have here is really a fractal type of astrology where specific historical or destiny patterns remain constant over different time scales.[8]

How the Maya used the 260 tuns of the "short count" and the 260 katuns of the Long Count in their construction of history is only beginning to be explored. In *A Forest of Kings* Schele and Freidel describe how Maya kings staged battles, ascensions and other rituals around key dates in their calendar, dates that put their event into a symbolic relationship with historical events. Clearly, history was understood to be a pattern that repeated itself on many time levels and this knowledge was behind the conscious scheduling of events. In his book *The Mayan Factor,* Jose Arguelles has developed this idea of the Long Count being a form of the 260-day count on a large scale. In it he organizes and interprets world history in the context of baktuns and katuns and points out correctly that mankind is now approaching the end of the entire creation epoch. What this may mean for the inhabitants of this planet is the theme of this creative, yet unsubstantiated and controversial, piece of writing.

The Ages of the Aztecs

Although the Maya produced the most sophisticated time period astrology in Mesoamerica, the Aztecs had some ideas of their own, or at least ideas build on earlier Toltec knowledge. In several post-

Conquest manuscripts, and also on the face of the famed Aztec Piedra del Sol, is found the notion of a succession of ages or creations called "suns." While the various accounts do not agree in their entirety, the basic idea is that there have been four or five previous ages or creations. During each one a particular deity had rule and at the end of the period a specific kind of destruction occurred.

In the account found in the "Leyenda de los Soles" (Legend of the Sun), a total of four creations (the present being the fifth) are described.[9] According to this native chronicle of the founding of the Earth, the first age, or "sun" as it is called, began in the year -955, in the Western calendar. This era lasted 676 years and was called 4-Ocelot. The people who lived during this time were eaten by ocelots (or jaguars) during the year 1-Reed on the day 4-Ocelot. The next "sun," called 4- Wind, began in -279. Ultimately, everything that existed during this age was carried away by the wind in the year 12-Serpent on the day 4-Wind. This age of Wind lasted 364 years which brings us to +85 and the beginning of the era 4-Rain. Again, total destruction occurred this time in the form of a rain of fire. The date of this destruction was the year 7-Knife, day 4-Rain. (One interesting sidelight of this period is that those who perished became turkeys). The next period, 312 years later and named 4-Water, began in +397. During this period it rained for 52 years and all perished in the year 4-Flower on the day 4- Water. This was another long period (676 years) which brings us to +1073 and the beginning of the fifth "sun" called 4-Earthquake. The account reports that under this "sun" the end will come with earthquakes and hunger.

One of the interesting things about this account is in the length of the various ages. All of the periods are multiples of 52 years, the length of the Aztec calendar round, the minimal coincidence period of the civil and sacred calendars. The longest period, which occurs in the first and fourth periods, 676 years, is 13 x 52, the number 13 being perhaps the most cosmic number to the ancient Mesoamericans. The other figures are 7 x 52 = 364 and 6 x 52 = 312. The ages, named after specific day signs, do not follow an obvious pattern in the sequence of the 20 named days.

While the account in the "Leyenda de los Soles" is more specific about the destruction of the ages, it shares with the other versions the

Figure 11. Peidra del Sol, in its entirety and a close up of its central area showing the five ages.

notion of the rulership of the periods. The first age, called 4-Ocelot, was ruled by the god Tezcatlipoca. When Tezcatlipoca was struck down by his rival Quetzalcoatl, the age of wind began. Tlaloc, the rain god, ruled next during the age of rain. During the age of water, the ruler was Tlaloc's wife, Chalchihuitlicue. The chronicles also concur regarding the beginning of the present era, the fifth "sun" 4-Earthquake. They tell of the gods getting together to start up the new age, and their decision that sacrifice was necessary. In the center of Mexico's Piedra del Sol (see Figure 11) is the face of Tonatiuh, the Sun god and ruler of the present age. Around the face are four squares each square containing the symbols of the four previous creations. The square at the upper right contains the glyph for Ocelot and four dots to designate that this marks the age of 4-Ocelot. Moving clockwise are the glyphs for 4-Water, 4- Rain, and 4-Wind. These four squares and the face of Tonatiuh comprise the outline of the glyph for Earthquake. In a circle around this configuration are the twenty day-signs.

In 1987 Jose Arguelles and others called for a great gathering of people to pray for the Earth. This "Harmonic Convergence" occurred on August 16th and 17th that year. The logic of this dating was suggested by both Mayan and Aztec cycles with help from Western astrology. It turns out that 1987 is five years before the last katun of the creation epoch (not so significant in my view) but it closes a series of nine 52-year periods since 1519, when Cortés began his invasion of Mexico. These are the nine "hells" that are said to be followed by thirteen 52-year periods called "heavens." The message was a good one, but the cycle logic is a bit tentative.

Chapter 8

Mars, Eclipses, Planetary Periods and a Possible Zodiac

Mars, Jupiter and Saturn

While the planet Venus and its motions are well documented in myth, the codices, and inscriptions, not much is known about what Mesoamerican astrologers thought of the other visible planets. One important bit of evidence is a computation table in the Maya Dresden codex that appears to be designed to track the movements of Mars.[1] The table itself is organized around the number 780, which is the synodic cycle of that planet. Amazingly, the 780- day synodic period of Mars is exactly the length of three 260-day counts and some have suggested that perhaps the table is just a Tzolkin manipulation of some sort. However, a strong link to Mars is supported by figures that are very close to the length of Mars' stations in the data in this section of the codex. A glyph of a snouted animal located in this table has been called by researchers the Mars-beast (see Figure 12). The table also singles out the day 3-Lamat as an important day for the planet, it being a computational entry point and possibly having an astrological meaning as well.

Recent interpretations of Maya glyphs on the inscriptions indicate that important coronation or dedication dates have coincided with planetary conjunctions. Schele and Friedel point to a number of these "coincidences," including a temple dedication in Palenque by a leader named Chan-Bahlum.[2] The inscriptions indicate that he apparently chose to dedicate his temples on July 23rd, 690 during a conjunction of the Moon, Mars, Jupiter and Saturn in the constellation Scorpio near the fixed star Antares, an event that must have been an impressive sight. Schele and Friedel interpret Chan-Bahlum's dedication during a such an alignment as an attempt to legitimize his claim to power.

The Maya appear to have perceived massive conjunctions as a kind of sexual union of the gods. In the timing of dedications and transitions in dynastic history, the Maya paid attention to these and other astronomical events, including planetary stations, appearance/disappearance points, and greatest elongation of Venus. A good example is shown in the astronomy of the day that Shield-Jaguar became king of Yaxchilan. The day was October 23, +681 when Jupiter was stationary going direct. Some years later, on October 28, 709, Shield-Jaguar and his powerful wife, Lady Xoc, performed a major bloodletting ritual on a day when Jupiter and Saturn were stationing just 2 degrees from each other in the constellation Gemini. These events are recorded in stone and are just two of many dynastic events that show strong correlations with planetary activity. Schele and Freidel recount many of these in their book *A Forest of Kings*.

Eclipses

The Maya also calculated the dates on which both solar and lunar eclipses could occur; a well-known table being found in the Dresden Codex. This eclipse table was identified by the prominence of the numbers 177 and 148, the number of days in six and five lunations. The table reveals that eclipses fall into only three roughly 40-day segments of the 260-day count. This is because two cycles of 260 days is equal to three eclipse half- years of 173.3 days. The Maya were intent on using the 260-day count as both a computer and a symbolic delineator and they found a good match with the timing of eclipses. By noting that eclipses would only occur during these three points in the cycle, they inadvertently discovered the Moon's nodes which would be at the midpoints of these 40-day segments. Once an eclipse point was verified, an interval of either five or six lunations would bring them to the next eclipse season. Although only one out of every four or five eclipses are visible in Mexico (less often with bad weather) there would be enough confirmation to commend the system.

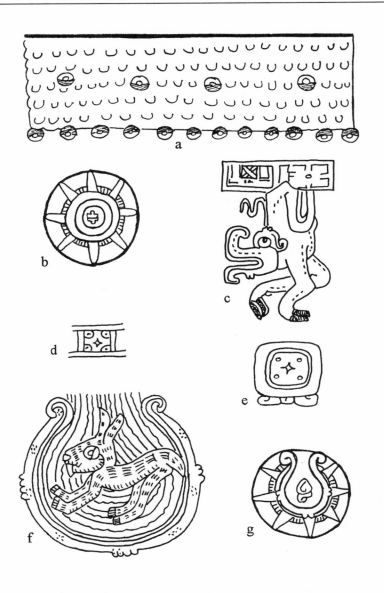

Figure 12. Mesoamerican symbols for celestial objects. (a) Stars, (b) Sun, (c) Mars, (d) and (e) Venus, (f) and (g) Moon

The Dresden Codex eclipse tables cover 405 lunations or 11,959.89 days. Again, a correspondence with the 260-day count is found here, 46 cycles of which equals 11,960 days. Most of the literature on the Maya eclipse tables is purely astronomical and not of exceptional interest for modern astrologers, but it is possible that the dates on which the eclipses fell, limited to just a few 13-day periods, may have held some astrological value for the Maya.

The Planets and the Day-Signs

Standard glyphs or symbols for the Sun, Moon, Venus and possibly Mars, figure prominently in the codices and inscriptions. Some of these are shown in Figure 12. Beyond these clear references are more subtle ones. Correspondences between the Mesoamerican gods, the day-signs, and the planets are suggested by the fact that the gods were often identified by a specific day-sign. For example, the goddess Mayauel, a Moon goddess, is also known as One Rabbit. The Moon in Mesoamerica was always portrayed as a rabbit because, like the Western notion of the "old man in the Moon," the darker shadings on the Moon were perceived as a rabbit. In this case we have the goddess Mayauel, the day-sign 1-Rabbit and the Moon linked together. Another example is Quetzalcoatl, associated with the planet Venus but also known as One Reed or Nine Wind. The dog-headed monster Xolotl, associated with Venus as an evening star, has the names Four Wind, Two House, Nine Serpent, Five Deer, One Earthquake and Five Flower. Other gods and goddesses also have multiple day-sign names. Is there a pattern to all this?

In an article titled "Astronomical Identities of Mesoamerican Gods," David H. Kelly argues that there is a complex internal consistency between the gods and astronomical facts embedded in the 260-day calendar. His thesis is that the distances (in days) from a specific point in the calendar to the calendrical god names equal real astronomical intervals for the planet that the god is associated with. His base date is 12-Lamat (Rabbit)/1-Pop, a single point in the 52-year cycle. In his article he shows how many of the calendar names of the gods and goddesses, counted from this base date, were equal to synodic cycles or lunar intervals. The implications of this thesis are that the 260-day calendar is also a device for storing astronomical information about the planets. It is a repository of cycle lengths. Confirmation for his thesis and his base date comes from a wide range of sources, the Aztec and Mixtec gods and legends, the Popol Vuh, and the Madrid Codex.

A few illustrations of Kelly's method should clarify this. First, he looks at Quetzalcoatl and notes the various calender names associated with this god, including the two mentioned above. Nine Wind in particular draws his attention and he notes that its position in the 260-day astrological calendar, #22 (see Table 2 in Chapter 9), is exactly 114 days ahead the base date of 12-Lamat or Rabbit. One Reed, another name for Quetzalcoatl, is exactly 115 days behind this base date. Kelly links this figure to Mercury's synodic cycle which is 116 days and suggests that, in this context at least, Quetzalcoatl is a god of the planet Mercury. It is with Quetzalcoatl's counterpart Xolotl that he finds correspondences with Venus. Noting that Five Flower is a name of Xolotl (as well as the Aztec god Macuilxochitl, god of pleasure, lust, and the ballgame tlachtli), he shows that its position in the 260-day count corresponds to one half of the Venus cycle. Five Flower is 33 days ahead of the base date 12- Lamat, but with one full 260-day cycle in between, it is 293 days ahead. The full Venus cycle is 584 days but the time between Inferior conjunction and superior conjunction is 292 days. Kelly argues that if 12-Lamat coincided with a superior conjunction of Venus and the Sun, then the following inferior conjunction would occur on the day 5-Ahau (Flower).

Another correspondence that is interesting involves Jupiter and Saturn. Kelly identifies these planets with the two principal gods of the underworld, Seven Death and Thirteen Death. These two dates in the 260-day calendar are spaced 20 days apart. So are the synodic periods of Jupiter and Saturn which are 398.8 and 378.1 days respectively. Subtracting 260 days from these figures, which simply accounts for one revolution of the 260-day count, Seven Death falls 139 days after the base date and Thirteen Death falls 118 days after it. Adding the elapsed 260 days to each, the resulting figures are 378 and 399, a remarkable correspondence.

Some planetary rulerships are suggested by using this approach. We've already seen how Quetzalcoatl, at least in his wind-god manifestation, may be the Mercury deity, while Xolotl is a Venus god. Jupiter and Saturn may be the gods Seven and Thirteen Death. These and other correspondences are listed below. The reader may refer to Kelly's article for more details and his reasoning behind these choices.

Mercury:
>Quetzalcoatl: Nine Wind, One Reed.
>Tlaloc: One Rain, Nine Rain.
>Tlaloc/Quetzalcoatl: Four Wind.

Venus:
>Xolotl: Five Flower, Nine Serpent.
>Macuilxochitl: Five Flower
>Chantico: Nine Dog.
>Hun Ahau: One Flower.
>Cinteotl: One Flower.

Mars: Mars Beast: 12 Lamat (Rabbit).

Jupiter: Vucub Came, Lord of Death: Seven Death.

Saturn: Black God of the Underworld: Thirteen Death.

Lunar Deities:

1. Node or Eclipse path Goddesses:
The Ciuateteo or God Women: Two Flower and Three Crocodile.
Old Moon God: Twelve Rabbit; Pot God:Seven Jaguar.
2. Old Moon Goddesses: Chicomecoatl: Seven Serpent.
Ilamatecuhtli: One Crocodile; Coatlicue: Twelve Reed.
Tlazolteotl: Six Reed and Nine Grass.
3. Young Moon Goddesses: Xochiquetzal: One Eagle.
4. Goddess of the Full Moon: Mayauel: One Rabbit.
5. Eclipse Goddess: Eleven Serpent.

A 13-Sign Sidereal Zodiac

In only a few places is there the barest of evidence that the Maya used a spatial zodiac likely composed of 13 signs. In 1916 the Mayanist Spinden commented on the sky-bands in the Paris Codex, suggesting that they might be a zodiac of sorts. Since that time others have broadened our knowledge about this aspect of Maya sky-lore and, through cross-referencing with stonework and murals, have filled in some of the blanks. The Paris Codex, while badly damaged at the edges, does contain drawings of 13 animals hanging from solar symbols beneath what is called a sky- band, the body of the celestial dragons (Figure 13). Entries in the computation tables in this section of the codex reveal repetitions of a 28-day interval. Since 28 x 13 = 364, the suggestion is that a kind of 13-sign zodiac is what is being described. Another testimony to this zodiac are the series of lintels on the Nunnery building at Chichen Itza that are reminiscent of this arrangement.

In his monograph on the Paris Codex, Severin (1981) lists the 13 signs and argues a number of points about them including the notion that they represent a sidereal zodiac. He suggests that the Maya knew about precession (which they probably did when you consider the length of the Long Count), and that they knew when the vernal point changed from sign to sign. He isolates the late 12th century BC as the time when the vernal point moved out of the second sign, a rattlesnake, and 862 AD as the time when it shifted into the sign of a dog or jaguar. Between these two dates, the vernal point traveled through a sign that is not clearly designated, but Severin notes that the interval between 1200 BC and 862 AD is the time during which Maya civilization developed and flourished.

Severin's list of the signs is taken in order from the Paris Codex and he sets them against the constellations in several diagrams.[3] At least half of the animals in this supposed zodiac are unclear or speculations. His order and naming of the signs in the Paris Codex is as follows:

1. Jaguar or Bird
2. Rattlesnake
3. Turtle
4. Scorpion
5. Bird
6. Fish-Snake
7. Vulture

8. Frog
9. Bat
10. Peccary
11. Deer
12. Death
13. Dog/Ocelot

Other researchers have challenged this straight-forward interpretation of the order of the alleged signs in the Paris Codex. It has been suggested that the signs lie at intervals of 168 days which would make them useful as eclipse tables since this figure is close to the

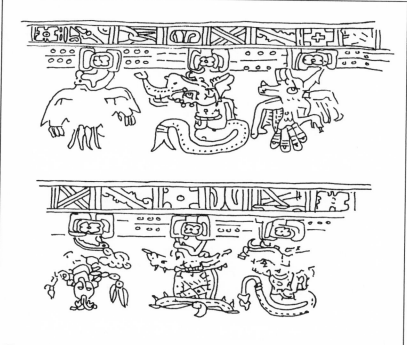

Figure 13. The sky bands with hanging zodiacal animals from the Paris Codex

eclipse half-year of 173 days. Bricker and Bricker (1993) point out that unlike Western astrologers who have always indicated the zodiac signs when they were invisible (when the Sun is in them), the Maya may have designated some of their signs when they were visible on the horizon, and that the sequence in the codex alternates between opposites. This may be the case as the Maya sign of the Scorpion appears to be the same as the Western constellation Scorpio and yet it falls adjacent to the sign Turtle which is known to be located in the constellation Orion. Bricker and Bricker's list and their constellational correlates are as follows:

2. Rattlesnake - Pleiades
3. Turtle - Orion
5. Bird 2 - Gemini
8. Frog - Leo (western portion)
10. Peccary - Leo (eastern portion)
11. ? - Virgo
1. Bird 1 - Libra
4. Scorpion - Scorpio
6. Fish-Snake - Sagittarius
7. Bird 3 - Capricorn
9. Bat - Aquarius
12. Skeleton - Pisces
13. Ocelot - Aries

The evidence for a Mayan 13-sign zodiac is scant and far from determining it as fact. Aside from the notion that the 13 sky beasts in the Paris Codex are a zodiac of sorts is the possibility that they represent the cycle of the 13 katuns. According to Paxton (1993), the tables in this section of the codex could have been used to locate solar positions at the beginning of the katuns. Paxton also points out that both the books of Chilam Balam and the Paris Codex indicate that each katun was linked to a specific constellation or group of stars. Like the badly damaged and only partially readable pages of the Paris Codex itself, and the confused and contaminated writings attributed to Chilam Balam, it is probable that the issue of a 13-sign zodiac will be never be settled -- unless some new evidence comes to light.

Section II:

Mesoamerican Astrology in Practice

Forward to the Second Section

The reader, after struggling with strange names and complex concepts, may be wondering if any of the elements of ancient Mesoamerican astrology actually work and are usable today. It is true that Mesoamerican astrological symbolism is based on the collective experiential and psychological themes of that culture and not those of Western civilization. The myth of Quetzalcoatl is not the myth of the Greek Venus. But because the astrology of Mesoamerica is founded on astronomical and numerological grounds that are common to all the world, the answer to this question is a definite "yes."

In the opinion of the author there is astrological substance to the 260-day calendar, as both a divinatory guide and personality type matrix. However, absolute proof that the system works is hard to come by. Those familiar with Western astrology know all too well that statistical testing of astrological premises is far more difficult than one would imagine. Aside from the 260-day astrological calendar, the phases of Venus and its potential malefic qualities should stimulate some revised thinking about the astrological qualities of this planet. Additionally, astro- historians and mundane astrologers may find workable possibilities in the katun cycle and the general concept of cycles that incorporate more than one astronomical phenomena. These are, at the least, interesting and worthy of serious attention.

In the introduction to this book the suggestion was made that the real value in an examination of an ancient astrological system lies in the insights it offers on the subject itself. In Mesoamerica, an astrology comparable to that of the ancient Mesopotamians survived until a mere 500 years ago, and some of it still survives. We can see how a culture attuned itself uniquely to the motions (both uniform and changing) of the sky. We can glimpse the beginnings of what would have become more of a horoscopic astrology, had the culture been allowed to evolve. While much has been lost, there are some salvageable elements, and the remainder of this book is dedicated to the those areas that may prove workable and useful to students of astrology.

Like the astrology of the ancient Near East, Mesoamerican astrology was mostly an astrology of the community and state, a kind of mundane astrology. Individuals did not have much free-will, they were chained to a wheel of destiny, actually the integrity of the collective, of which they were only a part. The 260-day calendar, the phases of Venus, and the cycles of the katuns were then universal sky and time symbols used astrologically by Mesoamerican society as a means of ordering and giving meaning to time and the rhythms of human life.

Except for the phases of Venus, eclipses, and a few other astronomical phenomena, the astrology of ancient Mesoamerica centered around specific time-periods based on astronomical cycles beginning with the day itself. Each block of time was symbolic; it had a specific meaning. It is possible that these periods, whether they be a day or 144,000 days took on their assigned meanings because they were part of the framework of the consensus reality of the Mesoamericans. Like a tarot spread, which presupposes that a particular placement holds a specific meaning, the ancient set of expectations molded the experienced reality of the population. The Western civil calendar and the work-day week, a major part of consensus reality today, holds a similar power over the modern individual which is both awesome and glaringly obvious. To be able to work against such consensus reality without experiencing stress and conflict, an individual would have to have acquired great personal power. Routines become habits, habits shape destiny. This reasoning gives a possible explanation for the apparently successful and reliable workings of the ancient astro-calendrical systems, which (one would suppose) would have been rejected by the culture if they didn't at least appear to work. It is certainly possible, as most academic researchers suppose, that clever astrologer-priests were fooling the public most of the time to maintain their position in the pecking order. This is not so far-fetched an idea, but a projection of current practice today, in the sense that those who have the truth podium (the scientists, academics, and politicians) force their views about reality on the public. We have been told "facts" that have later become false, as any careful study of the history of science will reveal.

An alternate view is that these ancient peoples discovered something of eternal importance, subtle rhythms in time that seem to have an effect on events and births. Like the three popularized biorhythms (discovered scientifically but still controversial), the pulses of 13-days and 20-days may actually have physiological correlates. As life on this planet has evolved, it has used environmental clues to establish survival strategies. Day and night create clearly defined states of consciousness that we call awake and sleep. Further, the cycle of the Moon appears to have been the "hook" that reproductive cycles in mammals became attuned to. Possibly there are profound causal connections between biological functions and the solar, lunar and planetary cycles. This theory may have merit, but few in the scientific establishment regard it as worth investigating; consequently there is no substantial research being performed in this area at the present.

Another important concept apparent in Mesoamerican astrology is that archetypal cycle patterns operate on different time-scales. The 260-day count is like the 260-tun "short count" and the 260 katun Long Count. Each of these units are in reality time-waves that resonate with each other. Mesoamerican astrologers saw history and destiny as constantly repeating itself on many levels, particularly when the numbers 13, 20, 52 and 260 were involved.

It has long been recognized that Maya astrologers worked to perfect their system, to join number science (numerology and fractal resonance) with natural rhythms. The effort to link the Venus cycle with the 260-day count in the Dresden Codex by way of periodic adjustments is a good example of this. They sought to understand the way the world worked and discovered that resonant time-frames (day = tun = katun) based around a few key numbers could be matched with planetary cycles. In a real sense, the Maya developed a kind of unified theory of how things worked and how they could be used. The Maya consciously adjusted their society to fit these forms, even accepting the collapse of their society if it fit the model.

In the next chapter and the pages that follow, the reader will find delineations, suggestions, and tables that should, hopefully, help to put Mesoamerican astrology on a firm footing in the modern age. Delineations for the day-signs, the 13-day periods, the Lords of the Night, and the Yearbearers are found in Chapter 9. Tables for the 260-day astrological calendar will allow readers to determine their birth sign in the calendar (Appendix A). Chapter 10 discusses the motions of Venus and its possible correlations with mundane and personal events. In Chapter 11, the katun cycles and their possible correlations with history, both Mesoamerican and Western, will be considered.

Chapter 9

The Astrology of Time

In Appendix A are tables giving a correlation between the Western calendar and the Aztec/Maya 260-day calendar. During the first part of the twentieth century a number of Maya scholars, archaeologists and astronomers, proposed various correlations, some differing by hundreds of years, yet each with its own rationale.[1] The fact that only one such correlation could exist is based on an assumption that a single continuous calendar was kept by the Maya during Classic and Post-Classic times and that no alterations occurred. Over the years, the Goodman-Martinez-Thompson (GMT) correlation has gained wide acceptance. The GMT locates the begining of the Long Count (start of the present age) on or near Julian day number 584,283. This correlation has an historical basis in inscriptions and also coincides within a day or two of the several post-conquest dates noted in both Maya and Western calendars.

One date recorded in both calendars was noted by Friar Diego de Landa who identified the day 12-Kan as July 16, 1553 (Julian calendar). Another is the surrender of the Aztecs to Cortes, given by several sources as taking place on August 13, 1521 (Julian) and the day 1-Serpent. This latter date agrees with the present day correlation of the 260-day calendar used by the Quiche Maya, but it is one day off from the date given by Landa. Using a computer program written by Barry Orr, I created an ephemeris for the 260-day count and analyzed the day-signs that occurred on the birthdays of personal friends.[2] It appeared to me that the correlation based on the surrender of the Aztecs and used by the Quiche Maya worked better than Landa's correlation. However, readers can do their own experimenting by simply shifting the day-signs ahead or backwards to see for themselves. A few years after I arrived at the conclusion that the 584,283 correlation "worked," a major academic work was published on Mesoamerican calendars, *The Book of the Year*, by Munro S. Edmonson. The author of this comprehensive survey on Mesoamerican calendars and their correlations, writes in his introduction "..the correlation constant of 584,283 is the only acceptable solution to the correlation question." There being agreement between astrologer and academic (though for totally different reasons) I feel confident about the tables printed here.[3] The correlation presented here places the zero date of the Long Count on August 11, -3113 (Julian calendar), which is the same as August 11, 3114 B.C.[4]

A second major correlation problem is in regard to what constitutes the begining of the day itself. There are conflicting indications that the day either began at sunset, midnight, or at sunrise. Some of present day Maya count the named days from sunset to sunset, at least this is what the anthropologists have observed. But the Maya of present day Yucatan start the day at midnight, and one could argue that this may be due to Spanish influence. Among the Quiche Maya, the arrival of the new year occurs at midnight. Calendar experts are known to hold important rituals on specific days and they begin their activities for these days at midnight.[5] In ancient times, the Aztec New Fire Ceremony, which occurred at the end of a 52-year cycle, was focused at midnight. Prior to this event all fires were extinguished. As the Pleiades culminated at midnight in November a man was sacrificed and a fire kindled on his body. The fire was then sent to other temples and eventually to the entire population. This turning of the ages at midnight is certainly a strong argument in favor of a midnight change of day. It was also recorded that Aztec merchants preferred to begin major trading expeditions on specific dates in the 260-day count. On these days, for example 1-Serpent or 1-Monkey, they would begin their activities with sacrifices made at midnight.[6] Finally, the issue of when the day began was never clearly documented in the early writings of the Spanish invaders, quite possibly because it didn't differ from their own Western methods in which the day began at midnight. In contradiction to this midnight starting point are Aztec and Maya myths that tell of the gods waiting for the Sun to rise and a new age to begin. Based on these myths, an argument for sunrise as the begining of the day might be made.

Readers can determine the day-sign of a birth, or any day, by turning to Appendix A. The tables in Appendix A assume that the day of the Aztecs and Maya began at midnight as it does today. Readers are encouraged to consider other possibilities. The author has noted that births occuring between 8 PM and midnight often display the qualities of the next sign. Quite possibly this is a transition period, a cusp of sorts. Readers should take into consideration time zones widely divergent from Central Standard Time, and also Daylight Savings Time.[7] These time adjustments, while not affecting all births, must be sorted out before a judgment on the 260-day calendar can be made.

Delineations of the Day-Signs

Below are summary descriptions of the the day-signs that are based on a combination of personal observations and logical deductions. I and others, having worked with these signs for a number of years, are of the opinion that they describe quite accurately the more salient features of a given personality. It has been suggested that the day-sign describes the persona or mask of identity -- in some sense it is like the Ascendant in Western astrology. Each delineation includes a short personality description, the sign's "challenge" and it's "solution." Also noted are correlations to Western astrology. The signs and planets listed as "astrology" are generally found to be quite prominent in the charts of those born under the day-sign. Other combinations are possible, in line with the general rulerships listed.[8] Following this are descriptions of the trecena, which seem to describe a deeper side of the personality, perhaps more like the Sun or Moon sign in Western astrology. For more detailed descriptions see my book *Day-Signs: Native American Astrology From Ancient Mexico.*

Alligator/Cipactli/Imix

Personality: Energetic, creative, and initiating.   Protective and dominating in a parental way. Sensitive and private.
Challenge: To become free from feelings of rejection, often from

parents.
Solution: Found a business or create a home.
Astrology: Cancer/Moon, Libra, Saturn, Neptune, Pluto.

Wind/Ehecatl/Ik

Personality: Communicative, mental, agile, clever, and multifaceted. Idealistic and romantic. Fashion conscious or artistic.
Challenge: Fears about responsibility, obligations, commitment, and decision-making.
Solution: Education and learning to communicate accurately.
Astrology: Gemini/Mercury, Pisces/Neptune, Saturn.

House/Calli/Akbal

Personality: Powerful, logical, organized, deep, thoughtful, and conservative. Good endurance, introspective.
Challenge: Mental rigidity and problems sharing feelings.
Solution: Become a builder of systems and establish secure foundations in whatever you do.
Astrology: Cancer, Leo, Capricorn/Saturn, Scorpio, 12th house.

Lizard/Cuetzpallin/Kan

Personality: Has strong emotions and feelings that affect others powerfully.
Challenge: To experience powerful transformations consciously.
Solution: Learning to accept change as part of the learning process.
Astrology: Aries, Scorpio, Leo.

Death/Miquiztli/Cimi

Personality: Security-conscious, materialistic, sacrificing, and helpful. Interest and concern for the community and politics.
Challenge: Having faith, not being a victim.
Solution: Give meaning to life by making contributions and sacrifices to society.

Astrology: Capricorn/Saturn, Scorpio, Pisces/Neptune, Moon.

Deer/Mazatl/Manik

Personality: Peaceful, generous, cooperative, artistic, and inspiring. Also nomadic, outspoken, and individualistic. Needs companionship and family.

Challenge: To handle the contradictory needs of personal freedom and relationship security.

Solution: To be comfortable with one's own individuality, no matter how strange it may be.

Astrology: Scorpio/Pluto, Taurus/Venus, Uranus.

Rabbit/Tochtli/Lamat

Personality: Energetic, busy, nervous, clever, and playful. Intelligent, but somewhat paranoid. Likes to fight.

Challenge: Keeping oneself under control in order to achieve completion. Focusing the mind.

Solution: Learning to express angry or competitive feelings constructively and avoiding extremes and excesses.

Astrology: Gemini/Mercury, Mars, Neptune, Aquarius.

Water/Atl/Muluc

Personality: Emotional, imaginative, psychic, romantic, and fantasy-prone. Strong desire nature. Dominates others easily by projecting strong feelings.

Challenge: Self-control and responsibility issues.

Solution: Being consistent, persistent, and intelligently responsive to emotional needs.

Astrology: Water signs, Neptune, Pluto, Moon, Mars.

Dog/Itzquintli/Oc

Personality: Cooperative, consistent, loyal and helpful. Good team player and joiner, but also good leader. Needs much variety and

mental stimulation in life.
Challenge: Reaching emotional maturity and dealing with father-related/authority issues.
Solution: Acceptance of leadership when it is needed.
Astrology: Leo, Scorpio, Taurus.

Monkey/Oxomatli/Chuen

Personality: Attention-getting, artistic, clever, and demonstrative. Multiple interests, communicative, and very curious.
Challenge: Perserverance in order to achieve mastery.
Solution: Many creative outlets and an active social life.
Astrology: Leo/Sun, Gemini/Mercury, Aquarius.

Grass/Malinalli/Eb

Personality: Relaxed, courteous, careful, and useful. Also sensitive, touchy, and easily hurt. Ambitious and hard-working.
Challenge: To avoid poisoning oneself by suppressing anger.
Solution: Expressing feelings, and fostering purifying and healing actions.
Astrology: Pisces/Neptune, Libra/Venus, Pluto, Mars

Reed/Acatl/Ben

Personality: Popular, knowledgeable, accomplished, and competent. A fighter for principles, a crusader. Takes on challenges.
Challenge: To not be opinionated, to loosen up rigid attitudes.
Solution: Knowledge of human nature and the development and exercise of good social skills.
Astrology: Libra/Venus, Sagittarius/Jupiter, Mars.

Ocelot/Ocelotl/Ix

Personality: Secretive, sensitive, intelligent, and psychic. Concerned with religion or spirituality. Aggressive but avoids direct confrontations.
Challenge: Complex and entangled human relationships.

Solution: Education and the development of counseling skills.
Astrology: Scorpio, Sagittarius, Aquarius.

Eagle/Cuauhtli/Men

Personality: Independent, ambitious, and escapist. Scientific, technically-inclined, critical, and exacting. Has unique ideas about life. Likes to make plans.
Challenge: Acceptance of unusual relationship patterns.
Solution: Cultivation of friendships that place a high value on personal freedom.
Astrology: Aquarius, Scorpio, Virgo, Moon.

Vulture/Cozcacuauhtli/Cib

Personality: Serious, deep, wise, realistic and pragmatic. Hardened to life, status-conscious. Sometimes dominated by others. Has very high standards.
Challenge: To overcome self-consciousness and personal insecurities through self-acceptance.
Solution: To excel in one's career and be comfortable with authority related issues.
Astrology: Capricorn/Saturn, Taurus.

Earthquake/Ollin/Caban

Personality: Mentally active, rationalizing, clever but practical. Usually liberal and progressive. Often controversial holding strong convictions and opinions.
Challenge: To hold one's life together according to a plan.
Solution: To become more flexible and patient.
Astrology: Aries/Mars, Gemini/Mercury, Uranus.

Knife/Tecpatl/Etz'nab

Personality: Practical, mechanically inclined, well-coordinated. Social, but struggles in close relationships. Compromising and self-

sacrificing, but suppresses anger.
Challenge: Self-interest versus self-sacrifice.
Solution: Cooperation and sharing with others.
Astrology: Libra/Venus, Aries/Mars, Capricorn/Saturn.

Rain/Quiahuitl/Cauac

Personality: Youthful, restless, friendly, and helpful. Multi-faceted, a good learner and teacher. Drawn to philosophy or religion. Concern for healing and purification.
Challenge: To become a healer of others.
Solution: Study under a master.
Astrology: Gemini/Mercury, Scorpio, Moon.

Flower/Xochitl/Ahau

Personality: Loving, devoted, artistic, dreamy, and romantic. Socially awkward but well-intentioned. Stubborn and uncompromising when ideals are challenged.
Challenge: Handling disappointments due to unrealistic expectations.
Solution: Being a good friend and keeping life simple.
Astrology: Libra/Venus, Pisces/Neptune, Capricorn.

The Day-Signs and the Directions

In Chapter 5 the order of the day-signs was shown to contain a number of internal arrangements, the most primary being the cycling of the directions east, north, west and south against the signs. With 20 day-signs, there are then five signs that come under each direction. When these are sorted out, an interesting pattern seems to emerge. In the view of the author, the directions, which are something like the elements (fire, earth, air and water) in Western astrology, underscore some fundamental differences between the signs, quite possibly pointing to a very basic level of operation or destiny.

East: The development of the individual. The personal dimension.
Alligator - personal centering and placement.
Serpent - personal power.
Water - exploring the emotional basis of the personality.
Reed - developing good judgment and facing life directly.
Earthquake - holding it all together; personal integration.

North: The development of the mind. The inorganic world.
Wind - learning, taking in ideas.
Death - playing by the social rules created by the mind.
Dog - creative thinking within the group tradition.
Ocelot - exploring the subconscious mind.
Knife - making decisions.

West: The development of the feelings. The organic world.
House - finding security and structure.
Deer - breaking the rules peacefully out of necessity.
Monkey - putting on a show, validating the self.
Eagle - perfecting judgement.
Rain - expressing emotion, using intuition.

South: Exploring the social world.
Lizard - sexual maturity and social integration.
Rabbit - competition; keeping in fighting shape.
Grass - living with compromise.
Vulture - finding one's place in the pecking order.
Flower - finding love and union.

The Trecena or 13-Day Periods

These 13-day periods act like signs in and of themselves. In the opinion of the author, they have a perceivable "influence" on public events and frequently a major theme of the sign will appear on the covers that week's national magazines. These blocks of 13 days are also worth looking at in terms of the astrological conjunctions, aspects, and eclipses that occur within them. In Chapter 4 you will find a listing of their influence according to Sahagun. The Western astrological symbols commonly found in the charts of those born under the trecena are very similar to those listed for the day-signs above. Readers are referred to those listings for suggestions about this matter.

1-Alligator/Cipactli/Imix

Beneath the surface personality is an emotional powerhouse. These persons have strong creative urges and feel an instinctive need to nurture others. For many, this is a desire to have a family to protect, though this need can also be met though pets and friends. Those born during this period can be very dominating, in an unconscious way, and others may have problems with this.

1-Ocelot/Ocelotl/Ix

Beneath the surface personality is an explorer of the human condition, a communicator, and a person who struggles with self-control. Critical events, such as deaths or other powerful transformations, may have caused them to turn inward and keep much to themselves. They need to be realistic about responsibilities because they tend to either shirk them or take on too many.

1-Deer/Mazatl/Manik

Beneath their surface personalities these people struggle with freedom versus security issues. There is an urge to take off for parts unknown, but also the desire for the security of home and family. Because the struggle with this conflict leads them to unique solutions, they often become innovators or creators of a somewhat unconventional personal lifestyle. Frequently, they have unusual interests that are of an investigative or searching nature.

1-Flower/Xochitl/Ahau

Beneath the surface personality lies a self that is very romantic and attracted to a glamourous lifestyle. Such a person may find success in life as a performer or as a "personality." Their greatest weakness is in matters of relationships. In this area they tend to be idealistic and often make poor choices that lead to many problems.

1-Reed/Acatl/Ben

Beneath the surface personality is a person who seeks constant self-improvement. Such people have a strong need to conquer their enemies and to achieve their objectives. While they make good teachers and role models, they also have a tendency to be somewhat self-righteous and overconfident of their own opinions.

1-Death/Miquiztli/Cimi

Beneath the surface personality is a strong commitment to the community. These persons will sacrifice time for others, though they are often not sure just why it is that they do this. They have an extremely strong sense of tradition and are attracted to history and antiquities. They are ultimately very down-to-earth people.

1-Rain/Quiahuitl/Cauac

Beneath the surface personality lies a self that is very dependent on others. Such people have a strong need to feel that they belong -- and feel part of a family. They also have an independent streak that often causes them to spend time alone, apart from others. In this respect, they experience many internal contradictions.

1-Grass/Malinalli/Eb

Beneath their surface personality lies a set of conflicting needs. Part of them wants to please, the other is a bit angry about all this compromising that they are expected to do. They have an interest in the deep, dark recesses of the world, the insides of people, and may do well in a career that allows them to legitimately explore such areas.

1-Serpent/Coatl/Chiccan

Beneath the surface personality is a person who struggles with powerful inner conflicts. This internal wrestling often leads to taking strongly committed positions on issues. When these people get going, they play hardball, and others may think them a bit fanatical at times, or somewhat extremist. They seem to know intuitively what they have to do in life -- even though they may not be able to express it logically.

1-Knife/Tecpatl/Etz'nab

Beneath the surface personality is a person seeking out powerful and transformative experiences. Such people are willing to go the distance in order to stimulate changes in themselves and in others. They are restless, and possibly a bit unstable; but they are persistent and quite devoted to their calling in life. At times, they will take risks that may even be life-threatening -- or they are attracted to others that do so.

1-Monkey/Oxomatli/Chuen

Beneath the surface personality is a strong need to be in the limelight, or at least to gain the attention of the public. There is something of the politician in them and they are instinctively attracted to activities like teaching, performance, and presentations of all kinds. They love to play and usually have several hobbies that keep them busy when they are not working.

1-Lizard/Cuetzpallin/Kan

Beneath the surface personality are strong needs for attention and recognition. The reactive self is creatively alive and seeks outlets for this energy. These persons are often leaders, often with some charisma. Others admire them for their confidence and willingness to take a stand.

1-Earthquake/Ollin/Caban

Beneath the surface personality is a dreamer. These persons have a fertile imagination and often find ways to make fantasy pay off for them. They may excel at one of the arts, or at least have a great appreciation for them. Their greatest assest is the ability to find ways to practically apply their ideas, bridging the gap from fantasy to fact.

1-Dog/Itzcuintli/Oc

Beneath the surface personality is a person who is very consistent in belief and loyalty. They will continue with a program or activity for years and can be an inspiration to others -- but they can also be extremely stubborn. Once they are committed to their lifestyle, no matter how unconventional, they are there for life.

1-House/Calli/Akbal

Beneath the surface personality is a deep need for very secure foundations. These security needs may be intellectual, as in science or religion, or they may be material, as in possession of valuables. Whether or not such persons seek mental or economic security, they are usually people with high standards to meet and uphold.

1-Vulture/Cozcacuauhtli/Cib

Beneath the surface personality is a person of strong will, not easily convinced by others. Such people have high standards and tend to keep themselves "above-it-all" and beyond criticism. They have a deep fear of rejection and are often troubled by guilt, both of these having a strong effect on their sense of self- worth. Most are quite talented though, or very knowledgeable, and have much to offer to the world. In some cases, however, they feel overshadowed in life by others.

1-Water/Atl/Muluc

Beneath the surface personality is a strong will propelled by powerful, irrational urges. These persons do things in life without a rational explanation -- just because they have to do them. They find it necessary to keep themselves under control much of the time, or they may risk offending others who don't understand them. They would be well advised to choose their friends very carefully for this reason.

1-Wind/Ehecatl/Ik

Beneath the surface personality are strong communication motivations. For some, this urge or interest may lead to a life of teaching or performing. Those born during this period are carriers of ideas; persons with a message to get across. They will always be instinctively drawn towards activities that will meet such needs.

1-Eagle/Cuauhtli/Men

Beneath the surface personality is a person with powerful faculties of discrimination. They know the differences between things, know how to express such distinctions and are often outstanding at articulating their feelings and emotions, or at least focusing them through a creative or artistic project. They are also somewhat psychic and find that their unconscious is their best friend, once they know how to listen to it.

1-Rabbit/Tochtli/Lamat

Beneath the surface personality is a competitor and fighter. This aspect of character may not always be apparent to others -- until they get to know them well. They secretly love a confrontation and will take risks in life in order to create them. These people prefer a life of excitement rather than one of routine, and they should try to meet these needs in a non-destructive way.

Day-Sign Tests

In 1989 I compiled a list of friends, and close aquaintences I had known throughout the course of my life, and I noted the day- sign and trecena of each. It was apparent immediately that I had developed major relationships with persons born on only about a quarter of the signs. There were also many signs that were left blank on my list -- I had never connected strongly with anyone born under their influence. If astrology and the system of the day-signs didn't work, then one would expect to find an even distribution of friends and close aquaintences throughout these signs. To me, this was striking evidence that something was working here, that the day-signs did describe personality, and that I was (as everyone does) connecting only with specific psychological types. Anyone familiar with Western astrology knows that this sort of thing also happens with that system. I also noticed that I was apparently quite attracted to those born on the day-sign exactly 10 signs, or half-way, ahead in the sequence. This and other similar observations and ideas are found in my book *Day-Signs*.

In order to take my observations further, I decided to do a small-scale test of persons that shared a common characteristic. From the NCGR/ISAR research data bank [9] I obtained a list of entrepreneurs and calculated their day-signs. These were persons whom I figured were probably among the more dominant members of society, and with them I could see if dominance and assertiveness as related character traits would stand out in a day-sign study. The results of this small test confirmed my suspicions. With 138 entrepreneurs and twenty day-signs, there should be close to an average of 6.9 entrepreneurs per sign. The day-sign Serpent, however, had fourteen born under it while Dog only had two. This was certainly in keeping with the delineations that I had been developing. Water was also statistically higher than the others with 10 born under it. Other day-signs that scored low were Monkey, Reed, Ocelot, and Flower. When I looked at the sorting from the perspective of the trecena I found that 1-House, 1-Water and 1-Wind were tied at ten each, while 1-Grass had only three and 1-Dog, 1-Vulture and 1-Rabbit had four. Although this modest study does not meet rigorous scientific standards, I think it points out a potential direction for reseachers on astrology. If these day-signs can be sorted out by psychological trait, profession, or other criteria, and clear Western astrological signatures can be attached to them (which seems to be the case), then we should be able to create an interesting and statistically significant set of correlations between all three.

The Burner Periods and Critical Days

The idea of dividing up the 260-day calendar, as if it were a circle, into halves and fourths, and possibly even further segments, appears in what are called the burner periods of the Maya discussed in Chapter 5. Here the 260-day cycle was quartered into four segments of 65 days. The days that marked the beginning of these subdivisions were 4-Chicchan (Serpent), 4-Oc (Dog), 4-Men (Eagle), and 4 Ahau (Flower). These four days (noted with an asterisk in Table 2) represent the four directions, and they are preceded and followed by days that inititated and closed the ceremonies concerned with their arrival and passing.

It appears from my research that when these dates come up in the 260-day count, local and world events reach critical proportions. In some cases crucial decisions are reached and in others tensions reach high levels. The public also seems to be deeply, almost compulsively, drawn to the news during these critical times. Normally, these kinds of trends are actually reached a few days before the burner date. It is interesting to note that the Maya had a 40-day preparation period, accompanied by rituals, for each of these points. Burning rituals may have been convenient ways for them to release accumulated tensions, and if these four dates do represent a kind of collective bio-rhythm, then the Maya were practicing a kind of collective preventative psychotherapy.

Applying the 65-day cycle to one's own day-sign works quite well in predicting critical points in life. Taking the number of a day-sign in Table 2 and adding 65 to it three times (subtracting 260 if the result is over 260) will yield four day-signs in the 260-day count that might be called critical dates. This is a quartering of the 260-day period starting with the day-sign of the birth. Experience has indicated that major personal events, trends or extremes tend to peak a few days before the arrival of each of these days. The effects seem to mirror the Western astrological notions of cycle division by four and the result is essentially two "squares" and an "opposition" to your birth day- sign. The arrival of the birth day-sign is quite personal and brings out strong feelings, the first quarter is active and demanding, the opposition day-sign (130 days later) is mental and deals with relationship and the third quarter is stressful mentally.

Delineations of the Lords of the Night

Not much is known about the 9 Lords of the Night. They are not a calendar per se, but a kind of symbolic cycle, which prompted my investigation of their possible astrological qualities. Whether these 9 deities (which appear in nearly all the astrological codices) rule hours of the day, hours of the night only, nights, or full days is unclear. We do know that the Maya had the Lords tagged to the Long Count and that on August 11, -3113 the ninth Lord was ruler. Starting from this date we can simply run a 9-day cycle along with the day-signs as is done in Table 1 in Appendix A. This table will allow you to determine the Lord of the Night for any day. As you will remember from Chapter 5, the Maya names of the Lords are lost but there is a complete Aztec list. These appear below in their usual order.

What the Lords of the Night actually mean in terms of personality or destiny is yet another matter. In the opinion of the author, the Lord ruling a particular day does seem to have an effect on at least some aspects of personality. Whenever the Lord of the Night and the day-sign are similar in nature (ie. Ocelot and Lord 8) the reinforcement of personality traits is quite pronounced. It is possible that the Lords may say something a person's darker and inner tendencies, or perhaps say something about one's unconscious life in general. The following delineations are based on personal experiences and may need to be refined a good deal before any last word is uttered.

Lord 1. Xiuhtecutli.

This Lord seems to have an influence similar to Mars in Western astrology. Persons born under it tend to be assertive, direct, and even combative. In some cases, they experience strong, forceful events in their lives as well. Interestingly, Xiuhtecutli is a fire god; Mars is synonymous with fire in many ways. Astrological correspondences seem to be Sun/Mars/Pluto combinations.

Lord 2. Itzli.

Itzli, the sacrifical stone knife god, seems an appropriate diety here because many of those born under this influence have strong Neptune placements in their Western birth charts. Neptune is a planet that represents loss of self and sacrifice. There also seems to be a theme of compulsiveness and even stubborness with those under this influence. This corresponds to the frequency of the signs Capricorn, Taurus, and Scorpio in the charts of those born with this Lord ruling.

Lord 3. Piltzintecutli.

Many born under this Lord seem to have prominent sense of self-importance. They are serious persons, perhaps a little insecure, but often in a prominent position in life. Some women born under it are married to someone who is powerful in the outside world. Since Piltzintecutli is a sun god, this seems appropriate. Sun/Saturn combinations are the Western astrological correlation.

Lord 4. Cinteotl.

Cinteotl is the corn god. Some born under the influence of this lord are teachers, some healers. Most seem to have an intensity about them, a nervous disposition, and a need to talk. Mercury is usually strong in the charts of those born under this lord, along with an emphasized 12th house.

Lord 5. Mictlantecutli.

Here, under the influence of the Aztec lord of death, we find persons who become deeply involved in relationships, or (just as often) struggle with them. They seem to be sensitive, even touchy, people who often have distorted opinions or over-inflated expectations about other people, often leading to disappointments. A prominent Moon, an emphasized 7th house, and Scorpio/Pluto are found in the charts of those born here.

Lord 6: Chalchiuhtlicue

Chalchiuhtlicue, the "Lady of the Jade Skirt," was the goddess of sudden storms. Although this suggests intensity, persons born on this day seem to be more often controlled, traditional, and markedly entrepreneurial. Mars and Saturn are often prominent in their charts, along with the sign Leo.

Lord 7: Tlazolteotl

Persons born under this goddess are strongly motivated by rela-tionships, partnering, and working with the public. They seem to be motivated by aesthetics, comforts, or material security. Tlazolteotl, "The Lady of Filth," was a confession goddess that "digested" a persons sins, particularly sexual ones. The common astrological signatures found in charts of those born on this day are a strong Venus/Libra emphasis and also the sign Virgo.

Lord 8: Tepeyollotl

This is the god of interiors, a jaguar god called "Heart of the Mountains." Those born here tend to have overstimulated minds and are often obsessive talkers, in some cases being counselors or psychologists. The planet Mercury, the sign Gemini, and an empha-sized 9th house are commonly found in the charts of those born here.

Lord 9: Tlaloc

People born under this lord are usually strong, independent characters, sometimes a little antagonistic. They are hard workers who prefer to work alone. Like Tlaloc, a major agricultural god of rain and water, those born on this day tend to have an emphasis on water signs in their charts as well as a prominent Mars.

The Years of the Yearbearers

As was discussed in Chapter 3, the problem of the yearbearers is complex because there has been a lack of consensus (even in pre-Conquest times) about which set of four ruled the years. The Aztecs used Reed (east), Knife (north), House (west), and Rabbit (south). If we start the year Reed with 1519, the year Cortes arrived, move in the order indicated above, then 1995 is also a Reed or east year. A different set of yearbearers are those used by both the Classic Maya and today's Quiche Maya. These are Caban (east), Ik (north), Manik (west), and Eb (south), which correlate with Earthquake, Wind, Deer, and Grass. According to the Quiche Maya, 1995 should be a year ruled by Eb, a south year.[10]

Considering the fact that the Quiche Maya correlation for the day-signs seems to work so well, one would think that their notions about the year might also be worth looking into. From my perspective, what is at stake here is the existence of a four year cycle, each fourth of which has a specific meaning. Four and eight-year cycles have been found in nature by cycle researchers, a strong suggestion that there may be a real material basis in the cycle of the yearbearers.[11] It is interesting to note that the Olympics and United States presidential elections are held in the same year, years that are ruled by the east, according to the Quiche. Further, the Chinese cycle of 12 years correlates with this pattern if you overlay that cycle with the 12 signs of the zodiac. The year ruled by Rat is thought by some to correlate with Aries. If this is so, then three 4-year cycles within the 12-year Chinese cycle each begin with a fire sign that correlates with the Quiche Caban or Earthquake, a sign of the east.[12] Although this is hardly enough proof that the Quiche and Classic Maya system is the one that works, it is a strong suggestion. There is a listing of these years in Table 3, in Appendix A. Following the year is the number that correponds to the year, from 1 to 13, according the Quiche tradition. Four cycles of 13 make up the 52-year calendar round, called Xiuhmolpilli by the Aztecs.[13]

Delineations of the Years

As with the Lords of the Night, we are on shaky ground here. First of all there is the big question of when the year begins. The Aztec year started in March, probably somewhere near the Vernal Equinox. The Quiche year also starts in March, but early in the month. The Postclassic Maya year started in July, but this was a moving starting point, one based on the fact that their calendar lost one day every four years. [14] If we accept that the years cycle direction-wise according to the tables above, we should begin an interpretation by considering traditional lore. Below is a list of Quiche Maya and Aztec notions about the years and their directional rulers.[1]

	Quiche	Aztec
East	creative/mental	fertile/abundant
North	violent weather	barren/dry/cold
West	wild/losses/illne	cloudy/evil
South	good business/health	variable

One can see that there is a general agreement between these two systems. Years ruled by the east and south are regarded as more positive than those ruled by the north and west. This is in keeping with the general, even worldwide, notions about the directions themselves, where east is spring, north winter, west autumn, and south summer. In the northern hemisphere spring and summer are seasons to look forward to, especially if you are living on a basic survival level. The delineations that follow are speculative and reflect both traditional ideas and general observations. It is quite possible that the number correlations in Appendix A (Table 3) will provide additional detail, as do the numbers of the day-signs. Low numbers are more forceful, high numbers are more matured, and 7 is the midpoint.

Years ruled by the East

Those born on these years are self-starters, competitive, activists, and self-involved. They work hard at being progressive and they often stand at the forefront of a movement.

Years ruled by the North

Persons born in these years are more mental and rational, this often keeping them (being in denial) from doing the things they should be doing. They are precise and exacting and are good problem solvers.

Years ruled by the West

Relatedness is a challenge for those born during these years. Skillfullness in dealing with people, diplomacy, and counseling abilities are their strong point. Indecisiveness is their weak point.

Years ruled by the South

The feelings and emotions of those born during these years are strong and have more of an influence over personal choices than do those born during north years. They can appear somewhat confused to others, or they can display unusual sensitivites.

Chapter 10

The Phases of Venus

For the Mesoamericans, the most important aspect of this planet's cycle was its morning star phase, particularly the first few days of Venus' morning visibility. At this point in its 584-day synodic period Venus rises just before the Sun and glimmers for a brief minute or two. The next day its visibility lasts somewhat longer, and within a week or two it rises well before the Sun and can be seen in the dark sky before the dawn. The day of its first visibility is called its helical rising, and this apparition was regarded throughout Mesoamerica as potentially dangerous.

As we have already seen, the Maya believed that when Venus rose before the Sun just after inferior conjunction it sent spears of light to earth and that these could strike down victims. In response to this belief, sacrifices were made and people would stay inside their homes to avoid gazing at what they called *Xux ek,* the wasp star. Some would even stop up their chimneys to prevent the light from entering their houses. Images of the god Kukulcan, who was associated with Venus and corresponds to the Mexican Quetzalcoatl, frequently show him spearing various victims. Just who or what Venus would strike depended upon the day of the 260-day calender on which the heliacal rising occurred.

Using an astronomical ephemeris, one can see that Venus makes its heliacal rising just after inferior conjunction with the Sun. This occurs while Venus is retrograde, about 15 days before it turns direct (also shown in the ephemeris). Venus is closest to the earth at this point in its sidereal cycle. Although there are variations due to latitude as well as atmospheric conditions, Venus will rise helically when it is roughly 5-7 degrees ahead of the Sun in longitude, which amounts to about 2 or 3 days after inferior conjunction. A listing of the dates of both inferior and superior conjunctions appears in Appendix C.

Does Venus rising before the Sun actually correlate with modern events that resemble the spearing and striking qualities ascribed to it by ancient Mesoamerican astrologers? An examination of the political events that occurred on or within a few days of the heliacal rising of Venus seem to confirm the idea of Venus being a destructive planet. In many, if not most cases, someone or something is struck down or being struck at. Power erodes and losses occur. Below are dates of Sun/Venus inferior conjunctions and some corresponding news events. We can assume that the actual heliacal rising of Venus occurred just a few days after these dates.

June 17, 1972: The Watergate arrests occurred on the 17th. Hurricane Agnes devastated the East Coast from the 18th to the 25th. Airline pilots from 64 nations staged a one day strike on the 19th.

January 23, 1974: A major plane crash occurred on the 31st.

August 27, 1975: On September 5th, Squeaky Fromme attempted to assassinate President Ford, and the government resigned in Portugal.

April 6, 1977: A Soviet fishing trawler that sailed into US territory was captured and later prosecuted by the United States.

November 7, 1978: The Shah of Iran's power was eroding rapidly and irreversibly. During this month he more or less allowed the military deal with the problems in Iran. The president of Bolivia resigned.

June 15, 1980: On the 13th and 18th some of the Abscam arrests were made. There were major riots in South Africa and Vietnam raided Thailand.

January 21, 1982: President Reagan announced his New Federalism plan in which the federal government would give the states less help. This was a major blow to state governments.

August 25, 1983: The Korean airliner 007 was accidentally shot down by the Russians on September 1st.

April 3, 1985: During this week, Ronald Reagan suffered a blow to his popularity by deciding to visit a certain German graveyard. He was also losing ground with other policies.

November 5, 1986: Within a few days of this date the Iran-Contragate scandal broke out, an event which discredited many in Reagan's administration and tarnished the president to some degree as well.

June 13, 1988: A few days later the government in Haiti was overthrown. On the next day a scandal of misuse of government money in the Pentagon was revealed. Two weeks later, the US Navy accidentally shot down an Iranian airliner flying over the Persian Gulf killing nearly 300 innocent persons.

January 18, 1990: Just after the inferior conjunction Washington D.C.'s mayor was busted on a cocaine charge. Mayor Berry was discredited and his political career left in shambles. On the 24th, oat bran, touted as a major health benefit, was also discredited, this time by scientists. A few days later a Colombian airliner ran out of gas and crashed on Long Island, killing many passengers.

August 22, 1991: Russian leader Mikhail Gorbachev was deposed by conservative party members. This event led to the downfall of the former Soviet Union.

April 1, 1993: A few weeks after this conjunction, on the day that the Moon transited its degree, the headquarters of a religious group called the Dravidians, who were resisting arrest, was assaulted by the FBI leading to the total destruction of the compound.

In the course of my investigation of this matter, it appeared to me that significantly more aircraft related news and also resignations or defeats occurred around the time of the heliacal rising than might be expected. In order to test this notion I attempted to tabulate selected news events with inferior conjunctions. I decided to concentrate solely on aircraft crashes that were listed in two reference books, "Darkest Hours" and "Chronicle of the 20th Century." Since not much aviation disaster data appeared before 1950, with the exceptions of the world wars, I limited myself to the 24 inferior conjunctions that occurred between then and 1986. Using the date of the inferior conjunction as a starting point, I counted major aircraft crashes that occurred within a 10-day period (which takes into account the actual heliacal rising of Venus), a 15-day and also a 20-day period.

Two sets of control dates were obtained in the following way. Using a random number generator set for numbers between 1 and 12, I generated two sets of numbers for each of the inferior conjunction dates. Calling each number a month, I added it to the inferior conjunction date thus arriving at a date within a year ahead that was used as a control date for aircraft crashes. For example, 1/26/66 is a date for inferior conjunction. Suppose the two numbers generated were 6 and 9, the control dates would be six and nine months later, or 2/26/66 and 10/26/66.

The results of this simple test confirmed my suspicions that more aircraft crashes occur on and shortly after inferior conjunction. There were 14 major crashes within 10 days of this event during period in question. The two control periods yielded 8 and 9 crashes. When the period was extended to 15 or 20 days, the number of crashes in both test and control groups were nearly the same. Since this test measures only major aircraft crashes listed in two reference books it is hardly scientific, but it does lend some support to my theory. Pilot error, what might probably also be termed bad judgment, was frequently given as a cause for the crashes that occurred near the date of the inferior conjunction. Perhaps there is a listing somewhere of all air crashes, large and small, with their causes, that could give this study more credibility.

Assuming that the heliacal rising of Venus has an observable effect on political life, it seems logical that it would have some effect on the lives of individuals. Suppose one were born on the date of a Sun/Venus inferior conjunction or a few days afterward at the heliacal rising of Venus? Would this indicate good or bad fortune?

Some research revealed the following. John Backe was born within a few days of the heliacal rising and his biography says he was a bomber pilot, quickly climbed the corporate ladder, and is known to keep things active. Another is the writer Ken Kesey, best known as a merry prankster who rode around the country during the 60's in a bus challenging people's values. Jack Nicholson was born just after the inferior conjunction and one could say that he causes a stir in people, at least through his films. I once read in Newsweek that his girlfriends call him "Spanking Jack," perhaps a reference to his version of the striking Venus depicted in the Maya codices. The skater Tonya Harding, best known for her involvement in an striking attack on one of her competitors, was born just three days after the inferior conjunction -- probably on the exact day of the heliacal rising. It could be said that those born at these times have (a) a "stimulating" effect on others, (b) may appear to be impulsive or even rash and (c) display or are involved with others that have strong sexual/territorial drives. In short, Venus in this part of its cycle seems a lot like Mars.

Most astrologers do not make a distinction between Venus as a morning or evening star. Dane Rudhyar, however, did so in his 1966 book "An Astrological Study of Psychological Complexes and Emotional Problems." In his section on Venus, he wrote about the dual role of Venus and its relationship to the emotional life. According to Rudhyar, Venus rising ahead of the Sun as a morning star signifies an emotional response that is impulsive, almost too eager to meet the world. This is a "young" Venus, exploring the emotional world in a naive and childlike manner. He called this phase Venus-Lucifer. As an evening star, which he called Venus-Hesperus, the planet signifies that personal emotional values and response patterns are strongly affected by social or cultural values, which can be a problem if these two sets of values differ significantly. This is a more cautious Venus, one that is less inclined toward emotional experimentation. Rudhyar considered the distinction between these two types of Venus very important in any understanding of the emotional life of both individuals and collectives, and he lamented the fact that few astrologers paid attention to it.

If Venus as a morning star, literally rising ahead of the Sun, actually implies emotion running ahead of itself, then the newsworthy events of the time should reveal such a trend. Again, based on my own pattern perception and not statistical research, I think this is so. Many of the plane crashes around the times of the heliacal rising after inferior conjunction were caused by pilot error or even aggression, as in the case of the Korean airliner. It appears that a high number of daring aviation or space-related feats tend to occur during this period also. Events during these times that led to resignations were mostly characterized by impulsiveness and wild risk-taking. Also, I found that candidates for high office that made their candidacy announcement during this period, generally did not get elected. Perhaps they were acting prematurely. Does this Venus heliacal rising period have any bearing on natal charts and does it act like a transit? I have observed that the houses ruled or occupied by Venus in natal charts often experience some jolts around this time. Regular routines are distorted and the flow of events tends to be more intense. Persons "ruled" by Venus sometimes suffer from emotional and often biologically induced upsets. I also think that persons born during this period have turbulent emotional lives, reflected in their love life. It appears to me that biological issues, including sexuality, the glands, reproductive organs, etc., are often a source of problems due to imbalances. Probably the simplest and most important lesson for astrologers is to make a clear distinction between the inferior and superior conjunctions of Venus and the Sun, and to pay special attention to the potential stresses and forceful qualities of the former. The effects of transiting conjunctions of the Sun and Venus will be shown in the areas of the chart that resonate with Venus.

Further insight into the nature of the inferior conjunction and the "newborn" Venus comes from the ancients themselves. In the mythology of ancient Mexico, Quetzalcoatl was the god linked to Venus as a morning star. He was the god who brought art, science, and culture to humanity, and was associated with the embodiment of civilized society itself, the ceremonial center. In the myths, Quetzalcoatl represents both a yearning for perfection and also a fall from grace through passion. It is at the heliacal rising of Venus that Quetzalcoatl descends to earth, commits a "sin" (becomes drunk and has sex with his sister), and is forced to face the consequences.

If Venus rising before the Sun implies risk-taking, impulsiveness, and breaking away from restraining influences in both myth and the news, what does Venus setting after the Sun mean? The Aztecs linked the animal god Xolotl with Venus in this evening star phase. Xolotl was depicted as a monstrous deformed animal with feet turned backwards. As the star that "pushes" the Sun into darkness, he was considered a being of misfortune. However, this phase of Venus seems to have been also considered favorable for ritual warfare. Possibly, as Rudhyar suggested, a kind of emotional repression or detachment may be characteristic of this phase. The control and power of the collective values that characterize this phase would be appropriate for activities that will not tolerate a personal, emotional outburst -- like successful warfare. But the constant inturning of personal emotion could produce a monster as well. One would suppose that this period "produces" fewer radicals and reformers than does the rising phase.

The following are delineations for the four parts of the Venus cycle as designated in the Mesoamerican tradition. Although, as we have seen in Chapter 7, the 584-day Venus synodic cycle was apportioned in sets of 8, 236, 90 and 250 days, this was apparently done for calculation purposes based on the lunar phase. See the listing of Sun/Venus conjunction dates at the end of this chapter to determine the appropriate phase of a birth.

Inferior Conjunction (+/- 4 days)

Because this phase of Venus lasts about a week, only one in 73 persons will be born during it. Those born during this period have very strong feelings and intuitions and are attracted to occupations where there may be considerable risk. At times they may be headstrong, upsetting others in the process and putting themselves into embarrassing situations. These are naturally creative persons that need to cultivate patience and restraint in order to realize their best ideas. They tend to be intense about sexuality, swinging from one extreme to another, excesses or abstinence. Their relationship needs are strong, but so is their need for freedom. In close relationships, they usually overpower their partner.

Morning Star/Venus Lucifer

This phase, which averages about 263 days, follows the Inferior Conjunction and precedes the Superior Conjunction phase. Persons born during it are like the Inferior Conjunction types in that they might be described as having "youthful" emotions and feelings. They are interested in the world and in other people and go out to meet them. They act first, evaluate later. Their warmth of feeling and willingness to join in with others makes them popular, unless others reject some of their more radical social initiatives. Ultimately, it is their feelings that move them to action and these feelings also allow them to make instant evaluations. Underneath it all they are individuals who test society's limits. Their personal vision is their purpose and motivation in life.

In their enthusiasm for life, they may occasionally make some mistakes. They need to remember to consider other's perspectives before putting emotional energy into actions based on instincts. These are creative persons who respond to a deep and very personal voice. In some cases, the rules of society may severely limit their initiatives, bringing the experience of defeat and disillusionment. Positively, with persistence these people may eventually succeed in impressing something of themselves onto the world, changing it for the better.

Superior Conjunction (+/- 25 days)

It appears that persons born in this phase have something of a struggle in life. Getting what they want is not easy, but a challenge. In the area of relationships major emotional problems arise, typically problems having to do with power and dominance. They struggle deep within themselves over what is right and what is wrong and, although they desire that there be peace in the world and in their relationships, this peace is not easy to come by. In order to move ahead in life they need to learn the lessons of defeat. Taking a loss can lead to a spiritual breakthrough, not just a loss of ego.

There is also a dark side to their personality that they find difficult to suppress. Their desire for power is strong and this pushes them to climb to great heights in life. Sexuality and violence are two themes that sometimes draw their attention, in movies and in literature. The darker side of human life is as important as the lighter side they need to face the darkness within themselves and befriend it, not stifle and alienate it.

Evening Star/Venus Hesperus

Following the Superior Conjunction, Venus spends about 263 days as an evening star. For people born during this period, feelings and emotions arise after an action has been taken. In making judgments, which they usually do very well, they evaluate what has happened against the background of society's rules and values. They instinctively understand the power, and perhaps the correctness, of the world as it is and has been. Their vision is one that has probably been strongly influenced by tradition.

One positive manifestation of evening star Venus is that they may become, consciously or unconsciously, successful due to the fact that they personify certain family and traditional values. In extreme cases, they become heros, people who represent what their society believes in. It is through participation with the traditions and cultural definitions of reality that they achieve emotional satisfaction and success in life.

Patterns of the Sun/Venus Conjunctions

Something the Mesoamerican astrologers were well aware of is the fact that Sun/Venus conjunctions, both inferior and superior, only take place in five distinct regions of the sky within a period of eight solar years. Over time these points move backwards against the fixed stars, completing a full cycle about once every 1,231 years. In the Dresden Codex are found five pages, each one dedicated to a cycle of Venus, that suggest the Maya astrologers distinguished between the astrological effects of each of these five stations of the planet. The Maya were able to locate these five Venus conjunction positions through the use of the 260-day count by focusing on the day-sign that came up when the inferior conjunction occurred. The mechanics of the interaction between the Venus cycle and the 260-day count are such that only five of the day-signs will occur at the time of the inferior conjunction. This was their way of predicting astronomical phenomena -- by reference to a time count. Western astrology utilizes blocks of space for the same purpose. Below is a list of Sun/Venus inferior conjunctions in zodiacal longitude from 4/6/1977 to 6/6/2012 grouped in five columns as in the Dresden Codex. (See Appendix C for a complete listing of Sun/Venus conjunctions.)

(1)	(2)	(3)	(4)	(5)
16Ar21	15Sc08	24Ge20	1Aq03	1Vi25
14Ar05	12Sc42	22Ge12	28Cp35	29Le15
11Ar49	10Sc18	20Ge03	26Cp07	27Le02
9Ar32	7Sc53	17Ge53	23Cp40	24Le51
7Ar16	5Sc30	15Ge45		

These five columns of Sun/Venus inferior conjunctions represent a Sun/Venus influence that moves backwards against the zodiac in time at a rate of about one zodiacal sign in 104 years. Although the conjunctions in each column occur at 8-year intervals, their movement over time can shown as a straight line graph through the zodiac and it appears that an astrological influence can be detected when this line crosses a sensitive point in the natal horoscope. This sort of graphic technique can also be applied to other planetary cycles of relationship.

The Mesoamerican astrology of the planet Venus offers many interesting insights into how this planet might be interpreted in a Western astrological chart. In addition to the distinctions between morning and evening star phases, and superior and inferior conjunctions, the specific family of conjunctions should probably be also taken into account for a complete analysis of Venus in a natal chart.

Chapter 11

The Cycle of the Thirteen Katuns

The Maya katun, a period of 7,200 days or nearly twenty years, was perhaps the most important of the long cycles in both Classic and Post-Classic times. Katun endings were major events, times for rituals and monument erecting. The ending of one katun and the opening of the next was very much a milestone, a changing of ages. Each katun had its own destiny or historical pattern, and in this section an attempt is made to analyze and possibly salvage some of what was once a calendrical rhythm of tremendous power.

The katun was composed of twenty tuns, or 360-day years, just as the uinal was composed of the twenty named days. In Chapter 7 it was pointed out that the period of the katun (19.71 years) closely approximates that of the Jupiter-Saturn cycle (19.86 years) to which past and present Western astrologers have long connected with social and political change. In the Maya Long Count or creation epoch, the period of time covered by thirteen baktuns (5125.37 years), contains exactly 260 katuns. The Maya creation epoch is simply one gigantic 260-day calendar, except that each "day" is nearly twenty years long.

In the writings of Bishop Landa and in the various books of Chilam Balam is found the notion of a cycle of thirteen katuns, sometimes called the "short count." If there are 260 katuns in a creation epoch, and twenty katuns in each of the thirteen baktuns, then there must also be twenty cycles of thirteen katuns in this period of time. The Maya Long Count has the katuns arranged in the same way as the Tonalamatl, in both twenty 13-katun periods and thirteen 20-katun periods. Because there is more documentation for the possible meanings of the thirteen katun periods, we will concentrate on these.

Each katun is named for the day on which it ends, and this is always the day Ahau (Lord), the Maya equivalent of the Aztec day Xochitl (Flower). This occurs because the length of the katun is evenly divisible by twenty, the number of the day-signs, so that it will always end on the same day-sign. Each katun is specifically named for the numbered Ahau day it ends on, that is the numbers 1 through 13 and the day itself (see Figure 10). Although the katuns are named for their last day, it turns out that the katun actually begins with the day-sign Imix (Cipactli/Alligator), considered the first of the day-signs. According to Landa, the cycle of the thirteen katuns begins with katun 11-Ahau which follows katun 13-Ahau, the numbers cycling in such a way that succeeding katuns are numbered two less than the previous one. If katun 13-Ahau ends on the day 13-Ahau, then katun 11-Ahau, the next one, must begin on the day 1-Imix, a fitting point to start the cycle.

Traditionally, during the course of a katun, a rulership change took place after the passage of ten tuns of 360 days. Apparently the patron god of the katun ruled alone for only ten years, and after that the god of the next katun shared it with him. Bishop Landa wrote:

"... they had in the temple two idols dedicated to two of the [katuns]. To the first..they offered worship, with services and sacrifices to secure freedom from ills during the twenty years; but after ten years of the first twenty had passed, they did no more than burn incense and do it reverence. When the twenty years of the first had passed, they began to follow the fates of the second, making their sacrifices; and then having taken away that first idol, they set up another for veneration during the next ten years."[1]

The cycle of the thirteen katuns is actually a cycle of 260 tuns (360-day years). Thirteen katuns, or 260 tuns, equals 256.26 years, a very interesting figure, for 258 years equals 13 Jupiter/Saturn synodic cycles. Also, 256 years is close to the amount of time needed for Sun/Venus conjunctions to precess 72 degrees, or 1/5 of the way, through the zodiac.[2] 256 years is also close to double the length of the Uranus/Pluto synodic cycle (254.98 years). What this means is that the Uranus-Pluto conjunctions will occur in specific katuns quite consistently over a long period of time. These turn out to be katuns 8-Ahau and 5 or 7- Ahau.

In the many books of Chilam Balam are found katun chronicles; events and prophecies of the cycle of thirteen katuns. Portions recount the history of the Maya in Yucatan during the age of Chichen Itza and Mayapan while other sections both predict and describe the conquest of the Maya by the Spanish. In some versions of the Book of Chilam Balam, the katun is said to be a period of 24 years, but these books, written well after the Conquest, are filled with popular European astrology and other contaminations. While the description of the meaning of each of the thirteen katuns is mostly allegorical and historical, there is still the notion that the same kinds of events occur whenever a particular katun occurs. This is an astrological view, that life moves in cycles and tends to form perceivable patterns. I have summarized these "delineations" below in order to test the possible use of this time-period kind of astrology.

Katun 11-Ahau: Apparently food is scarce during this katun and invading foreigners tend to disperse the population. There is an end to traditional rule, there are no successors. Since this is the first katun it always opens up a new era. It was during this katun that the Spanish began their takeover of Yucatan and imposed Christianity on the natives.

Katun 9-Ahau: This is a period of bad government where the ruler abuses his people and commits misdeeds. Rulers are so bad that they wind up losing some of their power to the priests. Carnal sin and adultery are practiced openly, by rulers and others, and it is also a time of wars. It is the katun of the "forcible withdrawal of the hand."

Katun 7-Ahau: This is apparently a time of social excess including drinking and adultery, a low point in the history of the society. Governments stoop to their lowest. The "bud of the flower," an allusion to eroticism, is said to sprout during this katun.

Katun 5-Ahau: During this katun of misfortune, rulers and their subjects separate -- the people lose faith in their leaders. Leaders may be harshly treated, even hung. There is also an abundance of snakes, a great famine, and few births during this period.

Katun 3-Ahau: This katun brings changes and calamities such as drought and wars. The people will become homeless and society will disintegrate.

Katun 1-Ahau: This katun brings even worse troubles, weak rulers and destruction. Governments fall apart due to rivalries. There may also be a great war which will end and brotherhood will return.

Katun 12-Ahau: Finally a good katun. During this period government and rulers are wise. Poor men become rich and their is abundance in the land. There is friendship and peace in the land. There will be six good years followed by six bad before well-being returns.

Katun 10-Ahau: Although this is a holy katun, there is trouble in the land once again. This katun brings drought and famine and is a time of foreign occupation, calendar change, and sadness.

Katun 8-Ahau: This may be the worst of the katuns as both Chichen Itza and Mayapan, the two great ruling cities of Yucatan, were destroyed during its period. The texts speak of demolition and destruction among the governors, an end to greed, but much fighting. It is the katun of "settling down in a new place."

Katun 6-Ahau: This is a time of bad government and deceptive government. There is also starvation and famine.

Katun 4-Ahau: There will be scarcities of corn and squash during this katun and this will lead to great mortality. This was the katun during which the settlement of Chichen Itza occurred, when the man-god Kukulcan (Quetzalcoatl) arrived. It is the katun of remembering and recording knowledge.

Katun 2-Ahau: For half of the katun there will be food, for half some misfortunes. This katun brings the end of the "word of God." It is a time of uniting for a cause.

Katun 13-Ahau: This is a time of total collapse where everything is lost. It is the time of the judgment of God. There will be epidemics and plagues and then famine. Governments will be lost to foreigners and wise men, and prophets will be lost.

This extremely depressing set of "predictions" leaves much to be desired. Out of thirteen katuns only one, katun 12-Ahau, has a positive reading, and perhaps katuns 4-Ahau and 2-Ahau could be construed to be somewhat positive. One would hope that clearer distinctions could have been made between the various katuns, but such is not the case and if any kind of astrological value is to be found here, we will have to find it through observation.

According to Landa, katun 11-Ahau was in its first year when the Spanish reached the city of Merida. This would be the year 1541. In the "Codex Perez and the Book of Chilam Balam of Mani" the prophecy of the priest Xupan Nauat states that the white men will come in the eighth year of katun 13-Ahau. Since the Spanish landed on the coast of Yucatan in 1527 this would suggest that katun 13-Ahau began eight years earlier in 1519 and katun 11-Ahau would then have begun in 1539. According to Makemson (1951) katun 11-Ahau began in 1535. While the dating of katun 11-Ahau is in the ballpark, there are some problems as an exact date for its beginning.

Assuming the GMT correlation is the authentic one, and since we know the time-span of the present creation age and its beginning and ending, we can simply divide it up into 260 katuns starting with August 12th -3113. The dates of katun beginnings for the past 800 years listed below were derived in this way. Notice that the 1539 date for katun 11-Ahau seems to be supported, once again suggesting that Landa's data is a little off. In the listing below the first number is the Ahau number that ends the katun, from which its name is derived. The beginnings of the baktuns, periods of twenty katuns, are also noted along with relevant astrological and historical data.

Katuns: 1027 to 2012

11   4.30.1027 "new era"
9   1.15.1046
7   10.2.1066
5   6.19.1086
3   3.7.1106
1   11.22.1125
12   8.9.1145
10   4.27.1165
8   1.11.1185   Conquest of Chichen Itza Uranus/Pluto (1200)
6   9.28.1204
4   6.15.1224   Beginning of baktun 12
2   3.2.1244
13   11.18.1263

11   8.5.1283   "new era"
9   4.23.1303
7   1.8.1323
5   9.27.1342 Uranus/Pluto conjunction (1343)
3   6.12.1362
1   2.27.1382
12   11.15.1401
10   8.2.1421
8   4.19.1441 Destruction of Mayapan, Uranus/Plutoconj.(1455)
6   1.4.1461
4   9.21.1480
2   6.9.1500
13   2.25.1520

11   11.12.1539"new era" - Arrival of Spanish (Montejo)
9   7.30.1559
7   4.16.1579
5   1.1.1599 Uranus/Pluto conjunction (1598)
3   9.18.1618   Beginning of baktun 13
1   6.5.1638
12   2.20.1658

10	11.7.1677		
8	7.25.1697	Final conquest of Itza, Uranus/Pluto	(1710)
6	4.12.1717		
4	12.28.1736		
2	9.14.1756		
13	6.1.1776		
11	2.17.1796	"new era"	
9	11.5.1815		
7	7.23.1835	Uranus/Pluto conjunction (1850)	
5	4.9.1855		
3	12.25.1874		
1	9.11.1894		
12	5.30.1914		
10	2.14.1934		
8	11.1.1953	Uranus/Pluto conjunction (1965)	
6	7.19.1973		
4	4.5.1993		
2	12.21.2012		

Beginning of baktun 0Glancing at the above list, a modern astrologer can see how the Maya must have gained great faith in this cycle. The Uranus/Pluto conjunctions take place consistently in katun 8-Ahau bringing with them revolutions and changes. Katuns 5-Ahau and 7-Ahau also contain these conjunctions, which interestingly occur in 1598 just before the beginning of a new baktun. It appears as if the Maya found a cycle of change and built a very clean and precise, mathematically cyclic formula to accommodate the phenomena.

The synchronicity of the katuns with the Jupiter/Saturn cycle is also reinforced. Although the katun does not exactly reproduce this cycle, it comes very close, and for long periods of time conjunctions and oppositions of these planets will fall close to the beginning of these periods. For example, the oppositions are presently occurring close to the katun beginnings.

Jupiter/Saturn conjunctions tend to occur in the same element of the Western zodiac for long periods of time. The change of element was called a "great mutation" and the change into Fire signs was considered to be particularly important. The last four mutations into fire signs occurred around -780, +14, 809, and 1603. The last seven baktuns began around -747, -353, +41, 435, 830, 1225, and 1618. Four of these match up fairly closely with the baktuns, supporting my argument that the katun cycle actually "works" in an astrological sense because it approximates natural phenomena.

Here is the list of katuns again arranged differently.

Katun #	Western years				
13 Ahau	1007	1263	1520	1776	2032
11 Ahau	1027	1283	1539	1796	2052
9 Ahau	1046	1303	1559	1815	
7 Ahau	1066	1322	1579	1835	
5 Ahau	1086	1342	1598	1855	
3 Ahau	1106	1362	1618	1874	
1 Ahau	1125	1382	1638	1894	
12 Ahau	1145	1401	1658	1914	
10 Ahau	1165	1421	1677	1934	
8 Ahau	1185	1441	1697	1953	
6 Ahau	1204	1460	1717	1973	
4 Ahau	1224	1480	1736	1993	
2 Ahau	1244	1500	1756	2012	

Looking at the dates of katun 13-Ahau, some substantial events can be noted. During the 1263-1283 period, the Hapsburg dynasty began its rise to power which it would hold for 600 years, and Marco Polo made his famous visit to China. Around the 1520 period, the Spanish conquered the New World empires and Luther set the Protestant Reformation in motion; events that have had lasting repercussions. The third date 1776, probably needs no discussion, at least to Americans, but this was also the period that included the French Revolution, the take-off point of the Industrial Revolution, and the discovery of the planet Uranus truly the beginning of a new era. The next katun 13-Ahau starts in 2032.

As we have already seen, the Maya considered katun 8-Ahau to be perhaps the most destructive of the series. The two great Maya cities, Chichen Itza and Mayapan, were both destroyed while this katun was in effect. Are periods ruled by katun 8-Ahau really destructive? Consider the summary below.

1185 to 1204

> Genghis Khan begins conquest of Asia.
> Shoguns eclipse Japanese emperors.
> Crusaders sack Constantinople.

1441 to 1460

> Turks attack and terminate the Byzantine Empire.
> War of the Roses, the struggle for the English throne.
> Turks conquer Serbia.

1697 to 1717

> Death of Charles II of Spain leads to chaos in Europe.
> Sweden under Charles XII attempts militant expansion defeated in 1709

1953 to 1973

> Cold war between USA and USSR.
> Chaos in Southeast Asia.
> Riots and protests during 1960s.
> China's "Cultural Revolution."

While it is true that many positive things happened during these periods, it does appear that katun 8-Ahau marks a time of change and instability worldwide. Perhaps this can be attributed solely to the Uranus/Pluto conjunctions that coincide with these katun years, but that is also the genius of the katun system it's in tune with natural cycles.

What about katun 6-Ahau, the one that follows katun 8-Ahau and is also the one we recently witnessed? The Books of Chilam Balam say that this one brings bad and deceptive government, famine and starvation. One could argue that during its course, between 1973 and

1993, there have been a few cases of deceptive government (Watergate, Iran/Contragate), we did have an actor for a president, and there has been an acute awareness of famines in Africa. The last time this katun occurred was between 1717 and 1736. During this period the "South Sea Bubble," a major business failure caused a financial panic, and in England, the old and young "Pretenders" continued to claim the throne. It was during another katun 6-Ahau, this one from 1460 to 1480, that the Spanish Inquisition was established and Lorenzo the Magnificent ruled Florence. Finally, katun 6-Ahau of 1204 to 1224 saw the Children's Crusade, an example of mass deception if there ever was one.

And what of the present katun? According to the Maya, the last katun began on 4/6/1993 and the Long Count/creation epoch closes on 12/21/2012. Following the scheme of the cycle of the 13 katuns, this is katun 4-Ahau. The Maya thought this katun brought scarcities and the arrival of great leaders. It was also the katun of remembering knowledge and writing it down. It does appear that in the past this katun coincided with a questionable measure of stability in the world and also significant advances in the written word. For example, katun 4-Ahau lasted from 1224 to 1244. During this time Frederick II took Jerusalem, but he took it diplomatically. The next time this katun came up was between 1480 and 1500. Clearly, this was a period of great voyages and discoveries but things were also relatively stable politically which made exploration possible. This period also marks an important period of growth in printing. Katun 4-Ahau came up next between 1736 and 1756. Interestingly, it was during this period that the first encyclopedia was published. The War of the Austrian Succession 1740-1748 did bring a settlement of territories and a measure of stability, and there were a number of alliances formed during this time as well. Power kept shifting, but did not erupt in an all-out way. Such may actually be the case from 1993 to 2012.

Finally, the present Long Count/creation epoch of the Maya comes to an end on December 21st (the winter solstice), of 2012. What will the katun that begins this new era be like? The Maya regarded katun 2-Ahau as half good and half bad, a time of uniting for a cause, but also as the katun during which came the "end of the word of God." And what does that mean? It is true that in previous

2-Ahau katuns there were great religious or ideological crises. Between 1500 and 1520 the Aztecs were conquered and eventually forced to convert to Christianity. Also in 1517 Martin Luthor started the Protestant Reformation. Between 1756 and 1776 the ideas of liberty and the rights of countries and individuals became a growing trend and this led to the American colonies declaring independence from England. One could say that a new era was indeed dawning, although it took a few more katuns before it could stand on its own two feet. Quite possibly some of our most taken-for-granted beliefs, secular and religious, will begin to lose cohesiveness and credibility after 2012, paving the way for a genuinely new age. If the Maya were right, then don't hold your breath for the mere millennium, the year 2000, hang on for the *real* changes that should begin twelve years later in 2012 and culminate with katun 13-Ahau which starts in 2032.

Aside from this division of the 5,125-year Long Count into 20 cycles of 13 katuns, we can divide the epoch in other ways. The division of this period into 13 baktuns (each totaling 20 katuns) was the usual way that dates were recorded in the context of the Long Count and these dates are listed below.

-3113	-2719	-2324	-1930	-1536	-1142	-747
-353	+41	+435	+830	+1224	+1618	+2012

Some of these dates to roughly correlate with important turning points in Western history, particularly +41 and the origins of Christianity and +1618 with the rise of modern science. Another way of dividing the epoch is simply to quarter it, and this produces some equally suggestive dates in history. These dates, starting with -3113, are -1832, -550, +730 and +2012. The midpoint of the epoch, -550, is particularly striking as this period was a time when many great teachers, including Confucius and Buddha, lived.

Like a biorhythm, which is the perfect form of a natural, though usually numerically inexact cycle, the katun allowed the Maya to better organize their life and to predict the future. Like a fractal wave, the Maya saw history as repeating itself on differing scales. With this knowledge they timed their rituals and gave meaning to human life. Perhaps we can use a few of their ideas.

	1	8	2	9	3	10	4	11	5	12	6	13	7
	2	9	3	10	4	11	5	12	6	13	7	1	8
	3	10	4	11	5	12	6	13	7	1	8	2	9
	4	11	5	12	6	13	7	1	8	2	9	3	10
	5	12	6	13	7	1	8	2	9	3	10	4	11
	6	13	7	1	8	2	9	3	10	4	11	5	12
	7	1	8	2	9	3	10	4	11	5	12	6	13
	8	2	9	3	10	4	11	5	12	6	13	7	1
	9	3	10	4	11	5	12	6	13	7	1	8	2
	10	4	11	5	12	6	13	7	1	8	2	9	3
	11	5	12	6	13	7	1	8	2	9	3	10	4
	12	6	13	7	1	8	2	9	3	10	4	11	5
	13	7	1	8	2	9	3	10	4	11	5	12	6
	1	8	2	9	3	10	4	11	5	12	6	13	7
	2	9	3	10	4	11	5	12	6	13	7	1	8
	3	10	4	11	5	12	6	13	7	1	8	2	9
	4	11	5	12	6	13	7	1	8	2	9	3	10
	5	12	6	13	7	1	8	2	9	3	10	4	11
	6	13	7	1	8	2	9	3	10	4	11	5	12
	7	1	8	2	9	3	10	4	11	5	12	6	13

Table listing all 260 day-signs as well as their positions in the trecena or 13-day count. The table begins at top left and moves down, one column at a time. (From Sahagun, The Florentine Codex, Book 4)

Appendix A

The 260-Day Astrological Calendar Tables

In order to find the day-sign and trecena of a particular date, first determine the number of days that have elapsed since the previous occurence of the day 1-Alligator/Crocodile using Table 1. Second, look up this number in Table 2 to find the named day itself, the number attached to it, and the trecena or 13-day period it occurs within. When determining the number of elapsed days, it may be necessary to take into account whether or not February that year had 28 or 29 days. Leap years, which have 29 days, are listed below.

Leap Years

1896	1920	1940	1960	1980
1904	1924	1944	1964	1984
1908	1928	1948	1968	1988
1912	1932	1952	1972	1992
1916	1936	1956	1976	1996
2000	2004	2008	2012	2016

TABLE 1

This table contains the dates on which the day 1-Alligator occurs between 1900 and 2012 according to the GMT correlation 584,283. Use this table to determine the number of days which elapsed between a given date, such as a birth day, and the previous occurence of 1-Alligator. Take this number to Table 2 to determine the day-sign and trecena of the date in question. The number in parentheses following each date in Table 1 is the number of the Lord of the Night ruling that 1-Alligator date. The examples below will help illustrate the two uses of this table.

Example 1. For a birth which occurred on 11/2/1955, the previous occurence of 1-Alligator was 8/4/1955. Counting the 4th as one, there are 28 days left in August, 30 in September, 31 in October and 2 in November. Adding these up gives a total of 91. An easy way to do this is to subtract the 1-Alligator date from the number of days in that month and add 1, then add the days of the succeeding months and finally the birthdate. Go to Table 2 to find that 13-Monkey is the day-sign and it is the last day of the trecena that begins with 1-Rain.

Example 2. For a birth that occured on 7/15/1960, the previous occurence of 1-Crocodile was 11/11/1959. Counting the 11th as one, there were 20 days in November, 31 in December, 31 in January, 29 in February (a leap year), 31 in March, 30 in April, 31 in May, 30 in June and 15 in July. The total is 248 days. Go to Table 2 to find that 1-Rabbit is the day-sign. Since 1-Rabbit begins the trecena that takes its name, it is also the trecena that influences the date in question.

To find the number of the Lord of the Night ruling any particular date take the total number of days between the date and the previous occurrence of 1-Alligator and subtract 1. Divide this figure by 9, take the remainder and add it to the number of the Lord that occurred on the previous 1-Alligator day. This is the number of the Lord of the Night ruling that day (or night).

Examples: In example 1 above, take the figure 91 and subract 1 which equals 90. Dividing by 9 equals 10 with no remainder. Add nothing to the number listed next to 8/4/1955, which is 2. The Lord of the Night ruling 11/2/1955 was therefore Lord 2. In the second example above, for July 15, 1960, the total number of days between that date and the previous occurrence of 1-Alligator was 248. Subtract 1, which equals 247 and divide by 9. The result is 27 with a remainder of 4. On the previous occurrence of 1-Alligator (11/11/1959) Lord #5 was ruler. Adding 4 to 5 equals 9. The Lord ruling 7/15/1960 is therefore Lord #9.

January 25, 1900	(9)	October 30, 1927	(5)
October 06, 1900	(8)	July 16, 1928	(4)
June 28, 1901	(7)	April 02, 1929	(3)
March 15, 1902	(6)	December 18, 1929	(2)
November 30, 1902	(5)	September 04, 1930	(1)
August 17, 1903	(4)	May 22, 1931	(9)
May 04, 1904	(3)	February 06, 1932	(8)
January 18, 1905	(2)	October 23, 1932	(7)
January 18, 1905	(1)	July 10, 1933	(6)
October 05, 1905	(9)	March 27, 1934	(5)
June 22, 1906	(8)	December 12, 1934	(4)
March 09, 1907	(7)	August 29, 1935	(3)
November 24, 1907	(6)	May 15, 1936	(2)
August 10, 1908	(5)	January 30, 1937	(1)
April 27, 1909	(4)	October 17, 1937	(9)
January 12, 1910	(3)	July 04, 1938	(8)
September 29, 1910	(2)	March 21, 1939	(7)
June 16, 1911	(1)	December 06, 1939	(6)
March 02, 1912	(9)	August 22, 1940	(5)
November 17, 1912	(8)	May 09, 1941	(4)
August 04, 1913	(7)	January 24, 1942	(3)
April 21, 1914	(6)	October 11, 1942	(2)
January 06, 1915	(5)	June 28, 1943	(1)
September 23, 1915	(4)	March 14, 1944	(9)
June 09, 1916	(3)	November 29, 1944	(8)
February 24, 1917	(2)	August 16, 1945	(7)
November 11, 1917	(1)	May 03, 1946	(6)
July 29, 1918	(9)	January 18, 1947	(5)
April 15, 1919	(8)	October 05, 1947	(4)
December 31, 1919	(7)	June 21, 1948	(3)
September 16, 1920	(6)	March 08, 1949	(2)
June 03, 1921	(5)	November 23, 1949	(1)
February 18, 1922	(4)	August 10, 1950	(9)
November 05, 1922	(3)	April 27, 1951	(8)
July 23, 1923	(2)	January 12, 1952	(7)
April 08, 1924	(1)	September 28, 1952	(6)
December 24, 1924	(9)	June 15, 1953	(5)
September 10, 1925	(8)	March 02, 1954	(4)
May 28, 1926	(7)	November 17, 1954	(3)
February 12, 1927	(6)	August 04, 1955	(2)

April 20, 1956	(1)	October 10, 1984	(6)
January 05, 1957	(9)	June 27, 1985	(5)
September 22, 1957	(8)	March 14, 1986	(4)
June 09, 1958	(7)	November 30, 1986	(3)
February 24, 1959	(6)	August 16, 1987	(2)
November 11, 1959	(5)	May 02, 1988	(1)
July 28, 1960	(4)	January 17, 1989	(9)
April 14, 1961	(3)	October 04, 1989	(8)
December 30, 1961	(2)	June 21, 1990	(7)
September 19, 1962	(1)	March 08, 1991	(6)
June 03, 1963	(9)	November 23, 1991	(5)
February 18, 1964	(8)	August 09, 1992	(4)
November 04, 1964	(7)	April 25, 1993	(3)
July 22, 1965	(6)	January 11, 1994	(2)
April 08, 1966	(5)	September 28, 1994	(1)
December 24, 1966	(4)	June 15, 1995	(9)
September 10, 1967	(3)	March 01, 1996	(8)
May 27, 1968	(2)	November 16, 1996	(7)
February 11, 1969	(1)	August 03, 1997	(6)
October 29, 1969	(9)	April 20, 1998	(5)
July 16, 1970	(8)	January 05, 1999	(4)
April 02, 1971	(7)	August 24, 1999	(3)
December 18, 1971	(6)	June 09, 2000	(2)
September 03, 1972	(5)	February 23, 2001	(1)
May 21, 1973	(4)	November 10, 2001	(9)
February 05, 1974	(3)	July 28, 2002	(8)
October 23, 1974	(2)	April 14, 2003	(7)
July 10, 1975	(1)	December 30, 2003	(6)
March 26, 1976	(9)	September 15, 2004	(5)
December 11, 1976	(8)	June 02, 2005	(4)
August 28, 1977	(7)	February 17, 2006	(3)
May 15, 1978	(6)	November 04, 2006	(2)
January 30, 1979	(5)	July 22, 2007	(1)
October 17, 1979	(4)	April 07, 2008	(9)
July 03, 1980	(3)	December 23, 2008	(8)
March 20, 1981	(2)	September 09, 2009	(7)
December 05, 1981	(1)	May 27, 2010	(6)
August 22, 1982	(9)	February 11, 2011	(5)
May 09, 1983	(8)	October 29, 2011	(4)
January 24, 1984	(7)	July 15, 2012	(3)

TABLE 2

This table lists the entire sequence of the 260 day calendar.
Using the figure determined from Table 1, find the
corresponding day and number. Also, move up in the table to
find the previous occurence of the number one, this being the
trecena that has rule over the following 12 days.

(*) Burner Dates

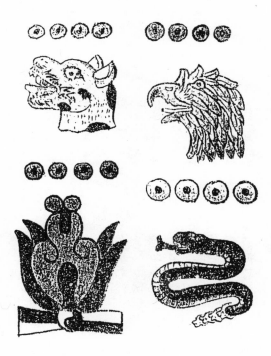

TABLE 2

1- 1 Alligator	14- 1 Ocelot	27- 1 Deer	40- 1 Flower
2- 2 Wind	15- 2 Eagle	28- 2 Rabbit	41- 2 Alligator
3- 3 House	16- 3 Vulture	29- 3 Water	42- 3 Wind
4- 4 Lizard	17- 4 Earthquake	30- 4 Dog (*)	43- 4 House
5- 5 Serpent	18- 5 Knife	31- 5 Monkey	44- 5 Lizard
6- 6 Death	19- 6 Rain	32- 6 Grass	45- 6 Serpent
7- 7 Deer	20- 7 Flower	33- 7 Reed	46- 7 Death
8- 8 Rabbit	21- 8 Alligator	34- 8 Ocelot	47- 8 Deer
9- 9 Water	22- 9 Wind	35- 9 Eagle	48- 9 Rabbit
10- 10 Dog	23- 10 House	36- 10 Vulture	49- 10 Water
11- 11 Monkey	24- 11 Lizard	37- 11 Earthquake	50- 11 Dog
12- 12 Grass	25- 12 Serpent	38- 12 Knife	51- 12 Monkey
13- 13 Reed	26- 13 Death	39- 13 Rain	52- 13 Grass

53- 1 Reed
54- 2 Ocelot
55- 3 Eagle
56- 4 Vulture
57- 5 Earthquake
58- 6 Knife
59- 7 Rain
60- 8 Flower
61- 9 Alligator
62- 10 Wind
63- 11 House
64- 12 Lizard
65- 13 Serpent

66- 1 Death
67- 2 Deer
68- 3 Rabbit
69- 4 Water
70- 5 Dog
71- 6 Monkey
72- 7 Grass
73- 8 Reed
74- 9 Ocelot
75- 10 Eagle
76- 11 Vulture
77- 12 Earthquake
78- 13 Knife

79- 1 Rain
80- 2 Flower
81- 3 Alligator
82- 4 Wind
83- 5 House
84- 6 Lizard
85- 7 Serpent
86- 8 Death
87- 9 Deer
88- 10 Rabbit
89- 11 Water
90- 12 Dog
91- 13 Monkey

92- 1 Grass
93- 2 Reed
94- 3 Ocelot
95- 4 Eagle (*)
96- 5 Vulture
97- 6 Earthquake
98- 7 Knife
99- 8 Rain
100- 9 Flower
101- 10 Alligator
102- 11 Wind
103- 12 House
104- 13 Lizard

105- 1 Serpent
106- 2 Death
107- 3 Deer
108- 4 Rabbit
109- 5 Water
110- 6 Dog
111- 7 Monkey
112- 8 Grass
113- 9 Reed
114- 10 Ocelot
115- 11 Eagle
116- 12 Vulture
117- 13 Earthquake

118- 1 Knife
119- 2 Rain
120- 3 Flower
121- 4 Alligator
122- 5 Wind
123- 6 House
124- 7 Lizard
125- 8 Serpent
126- 9 Death
127- 10 Deer
128- 11 Rabbit
129- 12 Water
130- 13 Dog

131- 1 Monkey
132- 2 Grass
133- 3 Reed
134- 4 Ocelot
135- 5 Eagle
136- 6 Vulture
137- 7 Earthquake
138- 8 Knife
139- 9 Rain
140- 10 Flower
141- 11 Alligator
142- 12 Wind
143- 13 House

144- 1 Lizard
145- 2 Serpent
146- 3 Death
147- 4 Deer
148- 5 Rabbit
149- 6 Water
150 -7 Dog
151- 8 Monkey
152- 9 Grass
153- 10 Reed
154- 11 Ocelot
155- 12 Eagle
156- 13 Vulture

157- 1 Earthquake
158- 2 Knife
159- 3 Rain
160- 4 Flower (*)
161- 5 Alligator
162- 6 Wind
163- 7 House
164- 8 Lizard
165- 9 Serpent
166- 10 Death
167- 11 Deer
168- 12 Rabbit
169- 13 Water

170- 1 Dog
171- 2 Monkey
172- 3 Grass
173- 4 Reed
174- 5 Ocelot
175- 6 Eagle
176- 7 Vulture
177- 8 Earthquake
178- 9 Knife
179- 10 Rain
180- 11 Flower
181- 12 Alligator
182- 13 Wind

183- 1 House
184- 2 Lizard
185- 3 Serpent
186- 4 Death
187- 5 Deer
188- 6 Rabbit
189- 7 Water
190- 8 Dog
191- 9 Monkey
192- 10 Grass
193- 11 Reed
194- 12 Ocelot
195- 13 Eagle

196- 1 Vulture
197- 2 Earthquake
198- 3 Knife
199- 4 Rain
200- 5 Flower
201- 6 Alligator
202- 7 Wind
203- 8 House
204- 9 Lizard
205- 10 Serpent
206- 11 Death
207- 12 Deer
208- 13 Rabbit

209- 1 Water
210- 2 Dog
211- 3 Monkey
212- 4 Grass
213- 5 Reed
214- 6 Ocelot
215- 7 Eagle
216- 8 Vulture
217- 9 Earthquake
218- 10 Knife
219- 11 Rain
220- 12 Flower
221- 13 Alligator

222- 1 Wind
223- 2 House
224- 3 Lizard
225- 4 Serpent (*)
226- 5 Death
227- 6 Deer
228- 7 Rabbit
229- 8 Water
230- 9 Dog
231- 10 Monkey
232- 11 Grass
233- 12 Reed
234- 13 Ocelot

235- 1 Eagle
236- 2 Vulture
237- 3 Earthquake
238- 4 Knife
239- 5 Rain
240- 6 Flower
241- 7 Alligator
242- 8 Wind
243- 9 House
244- 10 Lizard
245- 11 Serpent
246- 12 Death
247- 13 Deer

248- 1 Rabbit
249- 2 Water
250- 3 Dog
251- 4 Monkey
252- 5 Grass
253- 6 Reed
254- 7 Ocelot
255- 8 Eagle
256- 9 Vulture
257- 10 Earthquake
258- 11 Knife
259- 12 Rain
260- 13 Flower

Table 3

This table lists the cycle of yearbearers from which the name of each individual year is derived. There are two primary cycles at work here, a 4-year cycle involving the four directions, and a 52-year cycle during which time each direction has 13 years assigned to it. This version of the cycle of the yearbearers is the one used by the contemporary Quiche Maya of Guatamala. There were and are many different versions.

East	North	West	South
1900 - 5	1901 - 6	1902 - 7	1903 - 8
1904 - 9	1905 - 10	1906 - 11	1907 - 12
1908 - 13	1909 - 1	1910 -2	1911 - 3
1912 - 4	1913 - 5	1914 - 6	1915 - 7
1916 - 8	1917 - 9	1918 - 10	1919 - 11
1920 - 12	1921 - 13	1922 - 1	1923 - 2
1924 - 3	1925 - 4	1926 - 5	1927 - 6
1928 - 7	1929 - 8	1930 - 9	1931 - 10
1932 - 11	1933 - 12	1934 - 13	1935 - 1
1936 - 2	1937 - 3	1938 - 4	1939 - 5
1940 - 6	1941 - 7	1942 - 8	1943 - 9
1944 - 10	1945 - 11	1946 - 12	1947 - 13
1948 - 1	1949 - 2	1950 - 3	1951 - 4
1952 - 5	1953 - 6	1954 - 7	1955 - 8
1956 - 9	1957 - 10	1958 - 11	1959 - 12
1960 - 13	1961 - 1	1962 - 2	1963 - 3
1964 - 4	1965 - 5	1966 - 6	1967 - 7
1968 - 8	1969 - 9	1970 - 10	1971 - 11
1972 - 12	1973 - 13	1974 - 1	1975 - 2
1976 - 3	1977 - 4	1978 - 5	1979 - 6
1980 - 7	1981 - 8	1982 - 9	1983 - 10
1984 - 11	1985 - 12	1986 - 13	1987 - 1
1988 - 2	1989 - 3	1990 - 4	1991 - 5
1992 - 6	1993 - 7	1994 - 8	1995 - 9
1996 - 10	1997 - 11	1998 - 12	1999 - 13
2000 - 1	2001 - 2	2002 - 3	2003 - 4
2004 - 5	2005 - 6	2006 - 7	2007 - 8
2008 - 9	2009 - 10	2010 - 11	2011 - 12
2012 - 13	2013 - 1	2014 - 2	2015 - 3

Appendix B

A Reconstructed Tonalamatl

In Chapter 5 it was noted that a number of the surviving codices contain a listing of the 260 day-signs. The name for this listing was tonalamatl, meaning "book of fate." These listings are not generally printed in books on Mesoamerican astronomy because they are not strictly astronomical and they occupy a good deal of space. They are more like graphs that show the subtle inner structure of the amazing 260-day count. With one of these listings and a reference date, a Mesoamerican astrologer could find out when astronomical phenomena would occur, what signs were compatible with each other and when a critical day would arrive. The relationship between the day-signs, the trecena and the directions is obvious, but there are many more subtleties and potential uses.

The tonalamatl is a contained listing of the 260-day astrological calendar. Jose Arguelles has called it the "harmonic module" which is a most appropriate name as it can be placed, intact, into any number of astronomical cycles and used as a computer. Although this author uses the 584,283 GMT correlation between the Western calendar and the count of the day-signs, it is also possible to begin the count on any date at all and get useful results. In other words, the tonalamatl as a unit can be laid over the Western calendar and it will generate results because it will define and describe numerological relationships between days. Arguelles does exactly this as he uses a calendar correlation that is three months different than that used by the astronomers, archaeologists and ethnologists of the academic world and also the Quiche Maya of Guatamala themselves. However, in the opinion of the author, the real astrological value of the tonalamatl is found by using the GMT correlation noted above.

The Tonalamatl that appears on the next four pages is based on a type found in the Codex Borgia and the Codex Vaticanus B. In these tonalamatls, the day-signs are arranged in such a way that they must be read from bottom to top. In the Codex Borgia, the more artistic of the two, the reader must also follow the material from right to left. As this runs counter to the normal way that Westerners read, I have re-ordered the material so that it reads from right to left and top to bottom. Nothing else has been changed and this adjustment is totally superficial in terms of the purposes that the listing intended.

The four pages of the tonalamatl below display the 260-days in the following way. Page 1 is the region of the east. The first sign Alligator appears at the top left of a column of signs all ruled by the east. I have added the numbers from 1 - 13 in Maya notation along the top row. A dot stands for 1 and a bar for 5. The line beginning with 1-Alligator concludes with 13-Reed. To continue in the order of the day-signs, you must now turn the page to the section that begins with the signs of the north. At the top of this page you will find the day-sign 1-Ocelot, the day-sign that follows 13-Reed. Moving along this row you will finally arrive at 13-Death. Turn the page again and find the next sign, 1-Deer, at the top left of the page of the region of the west. Following the same routine, you will find 13-Rain at the end of the row and, after turning to the region of the south page, you will find 1-Flower, the next sign. Finally, at the end of this row is 13-Grass, and the next sign, 1-Reed, is found at the head of the second row on the first page, the region of the east. The order of the day-signs continues in this manner until all 260 day-signs are counted. Compare the arrangement of this tonalamatl with the listing of the day-signs in Table 2, Appendix A.

Besides the Aztec glyphs of the day-signs and the Maya numeration along the top row, there are enigmatic illustrations above and below each column. These drawings, mentioned in Chapter 5, were included because they do appear in both the Borgia and Vaticanus B tonalamatl, in nearly the same order with some exceptions. Seler (1902-1903), who was not sure what to make of all of them, pointed out that the figure that appears above the first sign of the directional region is the ruler of that segment, or at least sets the tone. In the eastern region, directly over 1-Alligator is an image of Quetzalcoatl. On the second page, over 1-Jaguar, is Tezcatlipoca. A female goddess with the mask of Tlaloc, and Tonatiuh, the sun god, rule the western and southern regions respectively. Interested readers, who have explored the mythology and iconography of the Aztecs, may find other correlations. In the squares containing the day-signs themselves are a number of footprints. These are spaced at intervals of 9 days and 7 days and have been suggested to fix the positions of the 9 Lords of the Night. A pair of dots at 3-Death is even more mysterious. The tonalamatl is a remarkable piece of numerological engineering that also fits natural astronomical cycles and invites exploration from those with a penchant for perceiving patterns.

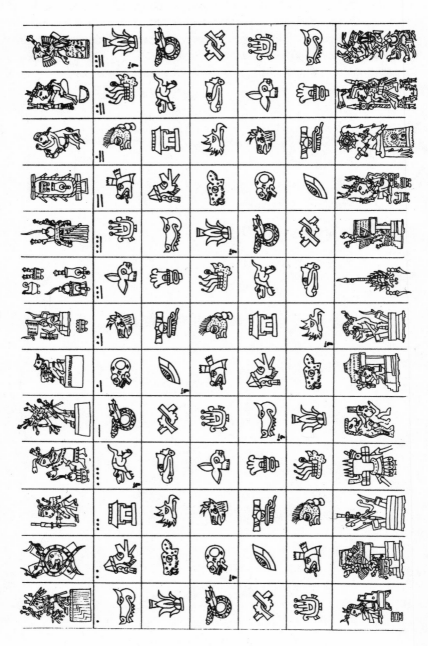

Region of the East

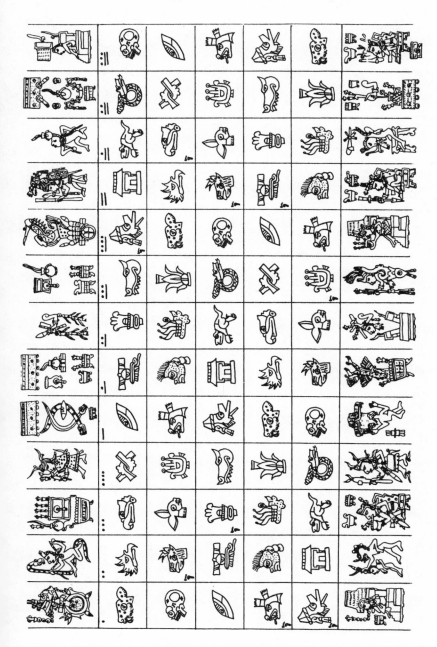

Region of the North

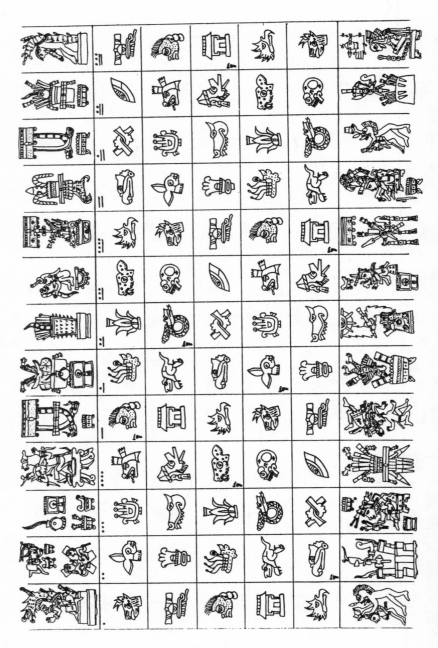

Region of the West

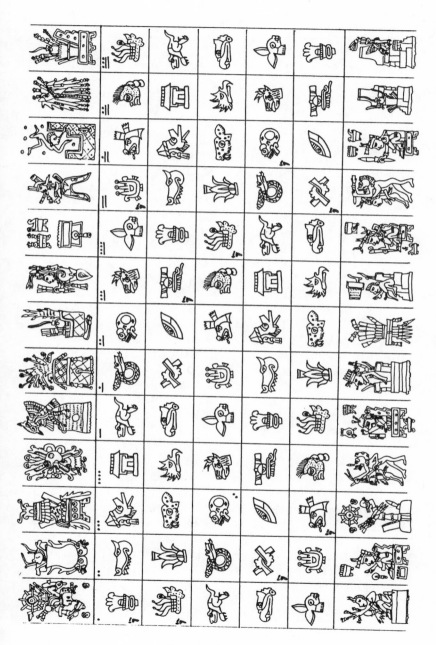

Region of the South

Appendix C:

Listing of Sun/Venus conjunctions: 1900-2012

Eastern Time
I = Inferior conjunction
S = Superior conjunction

7\8\1900	11:06	15Cn48	I	2\7\1926	15:11	18Aq06	I
5\1\1901	2:04	10Ta00	S	11\21\1926	12:29	28Sc27	S
2\14\1902	22:58	25Aq21	I	9\10\1927	17:54	17Vi01	I
11\29\1902	2:37	5Sg57	S	7\1\1928	15:34	9Cn31	S
9\17\1903	21:13	23Vi47	I	4\20\1929	9:27	29Ar48	I
7\8\1904	8:15	15Cn42	S	2\6\1930	17:42	17Aq14	S
4\27\1905	9:52	6Ta27	I	11\22\1930	18:18	29Sc44	I
2\14\1906	9:40	24Aq48	S	9\8\1931	4:13	14Vi33	S
11\30\1906	5:20	7Sg06	I	6\29\1932	4:41	7Cn12	I
9\15\1907	1:37	21Vi04	S	4\21\1933	16:23	1Ta06	S
7\6\1908	3:32	13Cn38	I	2\5\1934	4:26	15Aq41	I
4\28\1909	17:52	7Ta47	S	11\19\1934	0:21	25Sc59	S
2\12\1910	12:24	22Aq56	I	9\8\1935	8:51	14Vi46	I
11\26\1910	13:55	3Sg27	S	6\29\1936	9:45	7Cn27	S
9\15\1911	11:58	21Vi31	I	4\18\1937	1:15	27Ar36	I
7\6\1912	2:34	13Cn38	S	2\4\1938	4:07	14Aq42	S
4\25\1913	1:50	4Ta15	I	11\20\1938	6:32	27Sc17	I
2\11\1914	20:39	22Aq18	S	9\5\1939	21:16	12Vi24	S
11\27\1914	17:37	4Sg39	I	6\26\1940	21:15	5Cn04	I
9\12\1915	18:21	18Vi54	S	4\19\1941	7:37	28Ar51	S
7\3\1916	19:59	11Cn30	I	2\2\1942	17:34	13Aq15	I
4\26\1917	9:30	5Ta34	S	11\16\1942	12:10	23Sc31	S
2\10\1918	1:47	20Aq32	I	9\6\1943	0:07	12Vi32	I
11\24\1918	1:07	0Sg57	S	6\27\1944	3:59	5Cn22	S
9\13\1919	2:52	19Vi16	I	4\15\1945	16:46	25Ar21	I
7\3\1920	20:54	11Cn34	S	2\1\1946	14:22	12Aq08	S
4\22\1921	17:39	2Ta02	I	11\17\1946	19:04	24Sc50	I
2\9\1922	7:19	19Aq47	S	9\3\1947	14:26	10Vi14	S
11\25\1922	6:00	2Sg12	I	6\24\1948	13:39	2Cn55	I
9\10\1923	11:03	16Vi42	S	4\16\1949	22:51	26Ar36	S
7\1\1924	12:22	9Cn21	I	1\31\1950	6:43	10Aq50	I
4\24\1925	1:14	3Ta21	S	11\14\1950	0:01	21Sc03	S

9\3\1951	15:10	10Vi18	I	11\4\1982	2:03	11Sc19	S
6\24\1952	22:19	3Cn18	S	8\25\1983	4:36	1Vi25	I
4\13\1953	8:17	23Ar06	I	6\15\1984	22:34	24Ge58	S
1\30\1954	0:19	9Aq35	S	4\3\1985	22:02	14Ar05	I
11\15\1954	7:28	22Sc24	I	1\19\1986	16:06	29Cp18	S
9\1\1955	7:59	8Vi07	S	11\5\1986	10:18	12Sc42	I
6\22\1956	6:10	0Cn47	I	8\23\1987	6:26	29Le37	S
4\14\1957	13:41	24Ar20	S	6\13\1988	0:01	22Ge12	I
1\28\1958	19:49	8Aq24	I	4\4\1989	23:31	15Ar10	S
11\11\1958	12:22	18Sc37	S	1\18\1990	22:43	28Cp35	I
9\1\1959	6:24	8Vi05	I	11\1\1990	15:16	8Sc56	S
6\22\1960	16:27	1Cn13	S	8\22\1991	20:22	29Le15	I
4\10\1961	23:52	20Ar52	I	6\13\1992	16:32	22Ge54	S
1\27\1962	10:21	7Aq00	S	4\1\1993	13:12	11Ar49	I
11\12\1962	20:08	19Sc58	I	1\17\1994	2:04	26Cp44	S
8\30\1963	1:32	5Vi59	S	11\2\1994	23:12	10Sc18	I
6\19\1964	22:42	28Ge38	I	8\21\1995	0:05	27Le29	S
4\12\1965	4:23	22Ar03	S	6\10\1996	16:19	20Ge03	I
1\26\1966	8:39	5Aq57	I	4\2\1997	13:46	12Ar51	S
11\9\1966	0:41	16Sc10	S	1\16\1998	11:19	26Cp07	I
8\29\1967	21:42	5Vi51	I	10\30\1998	4:23	6Sc32	S
6\20\1968	10:24	29Ge08	S	8\20\1999	11:58	27Le02	I
4\8\1969	15:12	18Ar36	I	6\11\2000	10:32	20Ge48	S
1\24\1970	20:28	4Aq27	S	3\30\2001	4:17	9Ar32	I
11\10\1970	8:50	17Sc33	I	1\14\2002	11:32	24Cp07	S
8\27\1971	18:55	3Vi51	S	10\31\2002	12:07	7Sc53	I
6\17\1972	15:10	26Ge30	I	8\18\2003	18:06	25Le23	S
4\9\1973	19:15	19Ar48	S	6\8\2004	8:44	17Ge53	I
1\23\1974	21:21	3Aq30	I	3\31\2005	3:31	10Ar31	S
11\6\1974	13:10	13Sc44	S	1\13\2006	23:59	23Cp40	I
8\27\1975	13:12	3Vi39	I	10\27\2006	17:50	4Sc10	S
6\18\1976	4:38	27Ge04	S	8\18\2007	3:41	24Le51	I
4\6\1977	6:31	16Ar21	I	6\9\2008	4:20	18Ge43	S
1\22\1978	6:17	1Aq52	S	3\27\2009	19:24	7Ar16	I
11\7\1978	21:36	15Sc08	I	1\11\2010	21:06	21Cp32	S
8\25\1979	12:40	1Vi43	S	10\29\2010	1:11	5Sc30	I
6\15\1980	7:28	24Ge20	I	8\16\2011	12:09	23Le18	S
4\7\1981	9:24	17Ar28	S	6\6\2012	1:10	15Ge45	I
1\21\1982	10:08	1Aq03	I	3\28\2013	17:06	8Ar11	S

The above calculations were generated using NOVA software from:
Astrolabe, PO Box Box 1750, Brewster MA 02631.

NOTES

Footnotes to the **Forward:**

(1) A major effort has begun in the astrological community to translate all major ancient works on astrology into English and to retranslate those that have already been translated by academics but with little understanding of or sympathy toward astrology. This movement is called "Project Hindsight" and information about translations can be obtained from The Golden Hind Press, PO Box 002, Berkeley Springs, WV 25411.

(2) Aveni (1989), in *Empires of Time,* p. 228-229, elaborates on how historical time-keeping has been deeply conditioned by astrology and then, when it comes down to defining exactly what astrology is, he invalidates it by naming it religion. Presumably, because we know what religion is, astrology can then be dismissed. This is either bad analysis of data or a pathetic evasion and denial about the true nature of astrology coming from one of the greatest writers on historical astronomy.

Footnotes to Chapter 1: **The Prehistoric Origins of Astrology**

(1) Circadian cycles are daily cycles exhibited by life forms on this planet. Studies have shown that all kinds of organisms operate on a 24-hour (one earth rotation) rhythm, including the many individual systems that operate within the human body. A complex organism's ability to function actually depends on the close cooperation of many differing internal systems that beat or fluctuate on a daily basis. Life has internalized the rhythm of the day. (See Luce:1971)

(2) Geomantic construction or architecture attempts to harmonize a structure with its environment, including both the topographic and astronomic environments. The key concept is man in harmony with

nature, an idea that appears to have developed independently throughout the world. Environmentalism, as both a philosophy and activity, is the modern world's effort to re-attune itself with nature.

(3)   Tables of good times to fish or hunt are found in most fishing/hunting stores and magazines. It has long been common knowledge to fishermen and hunters that animals feed more intensely when the Moon is rising or setting. John Alden Knight's book *Moon Up-Moon Down* recounts how he spent a lifetime observing and perfecting a schedule for sportsmen based on the Sun and the Moon that he called the *Solunar Tables*. Hunters also know that the "Hunter's Moon" in autumn is the full Moon when deer are bolder and more aggressive and therefore easier to shoot.

(4) In the course of a 365-day year the Moon goes through its cycle with the Sun about 12 1/2 times. This is not a perfect fit by any means but it is probably the source of our present calendar with 12 months (moons) per year. Other societies, including the Hebrew and Arab, have kept the lunar calendar as the standard, but they add a month periodically to keep it in line with the seasons. (See Aveni: 1989)

Footnotes to Chapter 2: **Introduction to Mesoamerica**

(1) The sudden decline or collapse in the 9th century of the Classic Maya cultures of Mesoamerica is discussed in many textbooks. The reasons for the decline usually given by historians are overpopulation, excessive warfare, and belief in the ending of time. The collapse of Teotihuacan, which had strong trading ties with the Maya cities, may have initiated the decline.

(2) It was not until well after the Conquest that the name Aztec came into vogue. The conquistadors called them Mexicans, the friars simply Indians and natives. In some native histories it is told that they were originally from a place called Aztlan, but during their migration named themselves the Mexica (pronounced Meh-shee-ka, accent on the middle syllable).

(3) Book and library destruction was something also practiced by the Indians themselves. Sacking the holy place and its objects is the ultimate act of dominance, and it was common for a victorious

conqueror to seize the enemy's temple and destroy all the books and religious symbols. An example of this in ancient Western history would be the carrying off of the ark of the covenant of the temple of Jerusalem by the Babylonians (11 Chronicles 36:17-19), or more recently, Charlemagne's destruction of the Irminsul in his Christianization of the Saxons in 772 AD.

(4) These are the Dresden Codex, possibly the most complex and best preserved, the Madrid Codex which contains much astrological material, the Paris Codex, and the recently identified Grolier Codex.

(5) Published by Dover Publications as *Yucatan Before and After the Conquest.*

(6) Both the signs and houses of Western astrology represent or were originally derived from a quartering of space as determined by the Sun's yearly movements. The Sun enters the Cardinal signs, Aries, Cancer, Libra and Capricorn, on the days of equinox and solstice, and these dates are the key directional dates of the year. Aries and Libra occur only when the Sun rises and sets due east and west while Cancer and Capricorn occur when the Sun is at its greatest northern or southern extension, respectively. The houses are literally a local directional grid on which the planetary positions are placed. The Ascendant is east, the IC is north, the Descendant is west and the Midheaven south.

(7) An interesting diagram of these layers of space is found in the codex Vaticanus A. A reproduction of it can be found in Aveni:1980, p. 16.

(8) The 260-day period or count has been called by many names. Some astronomers and archaeologists call it the ritual almanac. Other names include ceremonial calendar, sacred almanac, sacred calendar and divinatory almanac. Jose Arguelles has named it the harmonic module. In this book it will be referred to as the 260-day count, the 260-day divinatory calendar or the 260-day astrological calendar.

(9) After 104 years or two calendar rounds, the synodic period of Venus (its "year" of 584 days) is brought into this interesting relationship of cycles. 104 solar years = 146 x 260-day divinatory years = 65 Venus years exactly.

(10) Precession is slow movement of the equinoxes against the fixed

stars. It is also reflected in the change of pole stars, Polaris being the pole star for our time, though not the pole star 5,000 years ago. It is due to a wobble of the earth's axis that such a cycle occurs.

(11) Sahagún, *Florentine Codex.*

(12) Bernal Díaz Del Castillo, who witnessed this event and wrote about it later, reported that, after a few months of cruising along the Yucatan coast and bothering the natives, Cortés arrived at what is now Veracruz on April 20th, Holy Thursday, in 1519 (Julian Calendar). Some Aztecs immediately approached the ship and made contact with Cortés. This date, the date of the first Aztec/Spanish contact, was not the day 1-Reed as some writers have suggested. Using the calendar correlation advocated in this book, the date would have been 6-Rain. However, a more formal meeting with a higher ranking Aztec, the governor of a nearby province, occurred on Easter Sunday which was the day 9-Wind, a day associated with Quetzalcoatl. This day is recorded by Aztec historians as the day that their troubles began. (Prescott: p.164 and Díaz: p.69)

(13) The name septimana first appears in the Codex Theodosianus, which dates from the 5th century. From this name comes the Italian settimana, the Spanish semana, and the French semaine (all meaning "week").

(14) Zerubavel (1985) argues that the Jews were the first to use the 7-day week as a cycle separate from natural rhythms, i.e. lunar, yet he also notes that this 7-day week came into being around the same time as the 7-day astrological week, which itself is also divorced from natural rhythms. Perhaps Zerubavel is simply trying to distance Judaism from astrology, which it was not so distant from in earlier times. See Aveni (1989), p.100 f. for a discussion on the 7-day week.

(15) The poem is astrologically correct. Lunar types (Monday - Moonday) often have fair, light and sensitive skin. Jupiter types (Thursday - Thor is the Germanic equivalent of Jupiter) like to travel. Saturn types (Saturday) are typically hard workers.

Footnotes to Chapter 3: **The 260-Day Astrological Calendar**

(1) Aveni:1980, p.148.

(2) A few surviving architectural structures contain zenith sighting

tubes that would allow an observer located deep within the building, or even underground, to sight zenith transits of the Sun or other astronomical body. Building P at Monte Alban is one example and the cave "Los Amates" at Xochicalco is another. Mexican astrologer Luis Lesur has reported that astrological charts cast for the moment of the Sun's zenith transits (there are two a year in Mexico) operate in some ways like an ingress chart. Perhaps locating the exact day of zenith transit was important as a means of forecasting in ancient Mesoamerica, just as locating the solstice and noting sky omens was, and is, important to the Pueblo and Hopi peoples of the American Southwest.

(3) According to New Jersey astrologer Jack Zanetti, the numbers 13, 20, 52 and 260 figure prominently in stock market fluctuations. These numbers can designate trading days, weeks or months and they specify the distance in time between highs or lows.

(4) Durán, p.398.

(5) Sahagún, Books 4 and 5, p.70.

(6) See Tedlock:1982.

(7) The first day of a civil year lasting exactly 365 days drifts backwards against the seasons at the rate of one day every four years. Although leap years can compensate for for this drift, they were not used in Mesoamerica. This was probably because leap years throw the year-bearer system off. Instead, larger adjustments after longer periods of time were used, or the drift was ignored. The Maya 365-day year drifted back against the seasons completing one cycle in about 1460 years. See Edmonson (1988) for the specifics on Mesoamerican calendars.

(8) Durán, p.392.

(9) Landa, pp.62-67.

Footnotes to Chapter 4: **The Twenty Named Days**

(1) In his book *Secrets of Mayan Science/Religion* Hunbatz Men (the founder of a Mayan Indigenous community in Mexico) reports that the letter "T" found on so many Maya monuments and writings symbolizes the Sacred Tree, the link between Man and God. Freidel, Schele and Parker (1993) have identified the Sacred Tree with the

Milky Way, the "T" being its crossing point with the ecliptic.

(2) Durán, pp.262-263.

(3) Sahagún, Book 7.

(4) There has been some confusion about the rulership of the day-sign Rain. Although the tonalamatls in the Codex Borgia and Codex Vaticanus B clearly show Tonatiuh as ruler of Rain, the goddess Chantico is linked with this sign in Burland's *Gods of Mexico* and also in Tunnicliffe's *"Aztec Astrology.*

(5) Durán, pp.399-404.

(6) Tedlock:1982.

Footnotes to Chapter 5: **The Tonalamatl or Book of Fate**

(1) Anthropologists usually define the word tonal as an animal guardian spirit, with the word nagual referring to a sorceror that could change into an animal. In Carlos Castaneda's book, "Tales of Power," his mentor Don Juan Matus describes the world as being divided into two parts, the tonal and the nagual. According to his definition, the tonal is the form that things take and the order of the world in everyday experience. It is also the social person, which is very suggestive when we consider the fact that the tonalli are the day-signs that symbolize personality and destiny in this world. The nagual, on the other hand, is the nameless reality behind the forms.

(2) There are two other Maya codices that include astronomical/astrological data: the Paris and the recently discovered Grolier.

(3) Arguelles:1987. .

(4) Sahagún, "Florentine Codex" Book 4.

(5) Burland:1967, pp.108-109.

(6) In Western astrology, the drekana are called decans. During the Greco-Roman period, the order of the decans reflected the order of the signs. Today, the order of rulership of the Hindu drekanas, also 10-degree segments, has become popular. In this system, the three decanates of any given sign are considered subsigns of the element the sign belongs to. For example, the first ten degrees of Aries is ruled by Aries, the second by Leo, and the third by Sagittarius, all of these being fire signs.

The important point here, however, is that there is a long tradition in astrology in which a sequence of symbols repeats on two or more scales. In the case of the Greco-Roman decans, the 12- sign zodiac is subdivided into three cycles of decans whose rulership follows the pattern of the larger unit. Essentially, this can be seen as three waves of the zodiac within itself. This is a kind of fractal situation where patterns remain constant over different scales.

(7) The burner periods are listed and described in Makemson (1951:75) and discussed by Thompson (1960:99-101).

(8) Thompson:1960, p.208 ff.

(9) Seler:1901, p.21 ff.

(10) The thirteen birds, as shown in the Codex Borgia, are, in order from 1 to 13: Dark Hummingbird, Light Hummingbird, Hawk, Quail, Dark Eagle, Screech Owl, Butterfly, Striped Eagle, Turkey, Skull Owl, Macaw, Quetzal, Parrot.

Footnotes to Chapter 6: **Quetzalcoatl and the Planet Venus**

(1) By "planetary astrology" I mean an astrology that is based primarily on the movements of the planets against a fixed background such as the zodiac. This is in contrast to a time-based astrology such as was predominant in ancient Mesoamerica and in the ancient Near East where the planetary hours developed. The origins of Western planetary astrology can be traced back to about -1600 during the reign of the Babylonian king Ammizaduga. Surviving records of the phases of Venus show not only that it was observed carefully, but that correlations of its phases with events were noted.

(2) Venus as anything other than a benefic is foreign to modern astrologers, yet such beliefs about this planet were held during ancient times in the Near East, the birthplace of Western astrology. The Mesopotamian version of Venus, while female, included warfare among her attributes. Lucifer was the name for Venus as Morning Star, and he (not her) was regarded as a fallen angel. Ancient Western astrological texts generally recognize the masculine qualities of Venus as a morning star and its feminine qualities as an evening star.

(3) The actual length of the synodic cycle can vary from little 581 days to 587 days.

(4) The figure of 4 days after inferior conjunction for the heliacal rising of Venus is not a constant. Latitude, time of year, and atmospheric conditions can all affect this interval. In an article called "The Arcus Visionis of the Planets in the Babylonian Observations" by C. Schoch (*Monthly Notes of the Royal Astronomical Society.* Vol. LXXXIV #9), the author notes fifteen actual observations of Venus' first visibility and reports a figure of about 5 to 6 degrees between Sun and Venus. These observations were made at the latitude of Babylon, roughly 35 degrees north. These figures of 5-6 degrees arc correspond to about 2 or 3 days after inferior conjunction, under the best viewing conditions. Most of Mesoamerica lies between 16 and 20 degree north.

(5) Sahagún: Florentine Codex, Book 7; p.11.

(6) This figure, 2,920 days is also very close to 99 lunations.

(7) Interestingly, 1/12th of 1231, the time taken for each of these conjunctions to precess 30.4 degrees or roughly one Western zodiacal sign, is 104 years. This is double the 52-year calendar round and equal to 65 cycles of Venus and 146 cycles of the 260- day count.

(8) See Aveni:1980, pp.258-277.

(9) Aveni:1992, pp.104-105.

(10) Thompson:1960, p.227.

(11) Codex Chimalpopoca, p.11. Also contained in Markman & Markman, p.368 ff.

(12) Seler:1902-1903

(13) Furst:1978, p.102 ff.

(14) Codice Chimalpopoca (1975), p.11, translation by author.

(15) Sahagún: Book 3 -- *Origin of the Gods*.

(16) Tedlock, D:1985, Popol Vuh p.234-235 and 296-297.

(17) Schele and Friedel:1990, p.444-446.

(18) See Schele and Friedel:1990 and Carlson:1991.

Footnotes to Chapter 7: **Maya Time Constructs and the Long Count**

(1) The Maya and Aztecs used a 365-day civil year that synchronized with the 260-day calendar in such a way that only four of the day-signs could fall on its first day. This 365-day civil year was

composed of 18 months of 20 days each plus five extra days. The
Maya name for this year was Haab, the Aztec name was Xihuitl.
Although the Aztec Xihuitl was probably tied to the seasons and had
to be periodically adjusted, the Maya Haab cycled with the 260-day
calendar, gaining one day every four years, and requiring 1460 years
to span the seasonal year. This is the same length of time as the
Egyptian Sothic cycle which was based on the slippage of the heliacal
rising of Sirius against the Egyptian calendar. See Jones:1982, p.77
ff.

(2) Landa, p.81.

(3) The Books of Chilam Balam are late post-Conquest writings
attributed to the "jaguar priest" Chilam Balam, who was either a man
or a title or both. They are written in Yucatec Maya language in
Spanish script and contain a mixture of traditional Maya calendric
and astrological material, European calendar dates, Western
astrology, weather prognostications, history, and the katun cycles. It
is possible that part of their contents are duplications of information
found in the much earlier hieroglyphic codices, but because they are
so contaminated, nothing is certain. Thompson (1960:p.297) calls
them "the sorry remnants of the old art of prognostication of the days
of the sacred almanac."

(4) Biorhythms (at least the three of 23, 28, and 33 days that have
become popular) are, in some ways, a Western version of day-
counts. Around the turn of the century, two independent researchers,
a doctor (Fliess) and a psychology professor (Swoboda) discovered
that periods of 23 and 28 days "fit" human activity rhythms and cell
cycles. The 33-day cycle came later. The case of the 28-day
emotional cycle illustrates my point. The period of the Moon, which
is about 27.3 days (synodic) or 29.5 days (sidereal) appears to be the
model for this cycle. Although the natural cycle is not a perfect
number, it is close to 28. Consider also the cycle of women's
menstural periods, which are rarely exact, but vary around 28 days.

(5) Some readers may immediately recognize this date to be quite
close to the starting date of the present Hindu Kali Yuga age said to
be February 18, -3102. This is also the approximate time that Menes
united the kingdoms of Upper and Lower Egypt, thus founding the
First Dynasty, and the time of the first cities in both Egypt and

Sumer. Furthermore, Stonehenge I, the original astronomically oriented circle, was built around this time in England.

(6) An example of the conventional Maya Long Count notation would be 9.17.10.16.3. This figure indicates that 9 baktuns, 17 katuns, 10 tuns, 16 uinals, and 3 kin have passed since the beginning of the present creation epoch (1,422,323 days since August 12, -3113). This is 3,894 years since that time or the date October 16, +781.

(7) The end date of the Long Count, 12/21/2012, is additional evidence that the Maya were cognizant of precession. John Major Jenkins (in *The How and Why of the Mayan End Date in 2012 A.D.* scheduled to be published in the December 1994 issue of The Mountain Astrologer) points out that the location of the Sun on this winter solstice date is right at the meeting point of the center (dark band) of the Milky Way (known to the Maya the "Road to Xibalba") and the ecliptic; precisely the point where the galactic equator meets the Sun's path in the sky. This crossing point was visualized by the Maya to be the cross of the Sacred Tree. In its roughly 25,695-year precessional journey against the fixed stars, the winter solstice point will be passing over this cosmic junction around 2012, the end date of the Long Count. Jenkins suggests that the ancient Maya calculated when this would occur and then built the Long Count around this highly symbolic astronomical punctuation mark.

(8) The notion that similar parts of Maya time units were in resonance is documented by Schele and Freidel (1990:252) in the patterns of kingship.

"To the Maya, days that fell at the same point in a calendar cycle shared the same characteristics in sacred time. Days that fell on the same point in many different cycles were very sacred indeed. By extension, events, such as births, which fell on days that were related cosmically, were also "like in kind." Because of the symmetry of their birth dates, Chan-Bahlum could declare that his father, Pacal, and the mother of the gods, were beings made of the same sacred substance."

Western astrology also has elements in which differing blocks of space or time share symbolic resonance. One example on the spatial level is the relationship between the decans or dwads and the zodiac (see footnote 6, Chapter 5). Another is the notion of a day equaling a year in secondary progressions. In this forecasting technique, the planetary aspects on each day after birth are said to resonate with the events in corresponding years of life. For example, if there was an opposition of Mars and Saturn six hours (1/4 day) into the 10th day after birth, there would be an event or trend symbolized by these two planets in the third month (1/4 year) of the tenth year of life. A third example is the use of half and double the solar arc in solar arc progressions. In this forecasting technique, the daily rate of Sun's motion in longitude after birth (again using a day for a year) is applied to each planet. This rate of motion is also halved and doubled creating two additional time frames that resonate with each other. For example, if the birth position of the Moon, moved at the rate of the solar arc, takes 10 years to reach Mars, an event or trend symbolic of the combination would occur at that age. The double solar arc would reach this point in half the time and the half solar arc in twice the time so that, in total, similar events would be predicted to occur at ages 5, 10 and 20.

For an interesting exploration of fractals and the zero point of the Mayan calendar see *The Invisible Landscape* by Terence and Dennis McKenna. *Timewave Zero*, a computer program based on that book, is published by Dolphin Software, 48 Shattuck Square #147. Berkeley, CA 94704.

(9) Codex Chimalpopoca, p.119.

Footnotes to Chapter 8: **Mars, Eclipses, Planets and a Zodiac**

(1) See Aveni:1980, p.195 ff.

(2) See Schele and Friedel:1990, p.256 and also pp.444-446.

(3) In his monograph, Severin presents a list of the signs and their positions in longitude corrected to 1950 AD. The list starts with the sign Jaguar which begins at 15 1/2 degrees of tropical Aries. The rest of the signs follow at 27.69-degree intervals (360 divided by 13).

(4) Aveni: 1992, Sky in Mayan Literature, p.167 ff.

Footnotes to Chapter 9: **The Astrology of Time**

(1) Entire articles have been written on the correlation problem. Good places to begin examining this critical issue are Aveni (1980) p.204 ff., Thompson (1960) p.303 ff., and Jenkins (1992) p.33 ff. Although the modified GMT correlation 584,283 is the generally accepted one, Floyd G. Lounsbury has challenged this in his analysis of the Dresden Codex and argues for a 584,285 correlation. See his highly technical paper in Aveni, *The Sky in Mayan Literature* (1992) for the details of his argument.

(2) After calculating a large number of day-signs for individuals, I noticed correlations between their Western astrological charts and the day-signs they were born under. I describe this process of discovery in my book *Day-Signs*. The program is used, written in 1985 and called Maya 1, has evolved into *Aztec-Maya Astro-Report*, a comprehensive program that prints pages of delineations for birth dates, does divinations, computes critical days, and handles complex calendar calculations and correlations. A "no-frills" version is also available. Both programs are available from Astrolabe (PO Box 1750, Brewster, MA 02631) or through One Reed Publications.

(3) Jose Arguelles, one of the originators of the 1987 Harmonic Convergence, uses a very different calendar correlation which he claims (in a personal letter) is based on the work of a Mexican artist. He uses the Post-classic yearbearers (Muluc, Ix, Cauac, Kan) with Ix ruling the year 1987.

(4) The Maya dated their cycles according to a zero, or completion date. August 11, -3113 is really more like what Westerners would regard as completion, the cycles of the previous age being all filled up on that date. The day-sign Ahau ruled that day and it is the last of the 20 day-signs. The next day, August 12, -3113, was the day Imix, the first of the 20 day-signs, and it could be said that the new creation epoch actually started on that day. The convention among students of the Long Count has been to regard the Maya zero date as the starting date even though the Ahau day-sign on that date gives its name to the previous, not the forthcoming, katun. In some of my writings I have

taken the next day as the starting date and that is what I have done in this book. Another example of this difference is the date of the most recent (and last) katun of the Long Count. This is April 5, 1993, when the day-sign was 6-Ahau. I specified the next day, 7-Imix, in published articles as the actual start of this katun. This current katun is named 4-Ahau because this day- sign will come up on its final day, December 21, 2012.

(5) Tedlock (1982) p.100-101. See also Thompson (1960) p.303 ff.

(6) Van Zantwijk (1985) p.152. The days 1-Serpent and 1-Monkey are spaced exactly 2 trecena or 26 days apart in the 260-day count.

(7) Most of Mexico is in Central Standard Time or time zone 6. It has been my observation that converting birth times to Mexico time yields better results. To convert, subtract one hour per zone if born east of zone 6, or add one hour per zone if born west. For example, someone born at 3 PM in Eastern Standard Time (time zone 5) would convert the birth time to 2 PM. Someone born in Pacific Standard Time (time zone 8) would add two hours arriving at a 5 PM birthtime.

(8) Aries and Mars represent similar energies and might be said to be symbolically interchangeable. Astrologer Zip Dobbins has promoted this working linkage between signs, planets and houses that resonate with each other.

(9) IDEA, the International Data Exchange for Astrologers, is sponsored by the International Society for Astrological Research (ISAR) and the National Council for Geocosmic Research (NCGR). This data bank has thousands of entries in over 300 categories that can be purchased for a small fee.

(10) Tedlock (1982) p.100. Eb is equivalent ot the Quiche E, or Grass. If this sign ruled the year 1975, as is indicated in the above reference, as well as every four years since, then it would also be the ruler of 1995.

(11) Dewey (1971) p.192-193. Is there a natural 4-year cycle? Dewey notes a number of 8-year cycles involving abundance, production, and value. These are:

Production: cigarettes, coal,steel, lead, cotton, iron, oil.

Abundance: whiting, lynx, red squirrel.

Value: butter, stocks, sugar.

Other: barometric pressure, precipitation, pine growth.

Dewey's charts show peaks at 1960 and every 8 years before and after. If this 8-year cycle is divided into two 4-year cycles, then the peaks and troughs correlate with the Quiche Maya and Chinese year cycles. Perhaps the election and olympic years are part of this 8-year cycle, with alternating east/fire years being either yin or yang compliments to each other.

(12) The Chinese have used a duodenary (12) year cycle since ancient times. The twelve branches (origins dated approximately -500) and the animal years (origins dated approximately +750) are similar and are correlated in many ways. The origins are obscure, but they may be based on the 12-year Jupiter cycle. Are they a zodiac, an extension of the offices of the day, hour names or monthy rites? If organized like the zodiac (and many sources link Rat with Aries and so on) then Rat, Dragon and Monkey would correspond with the fire signs. It does turn out that these signs rule the same years, the election and olympic years, as the east signs of the Quiche Maya. By overlaying the zodiac on this scheme, 1992 is ruled by Sagittarius, 1993 by Capricorn, etc., or 1992 is a east year, 1993 a north year, etc.

Rat Aries 1948, 60, 72, 84, 96 East
Ox Taurus 1949, 61, 73, 85, 97 North
Tiger Gemini 1950, 62, 74, 86, 98 West
Cat/Hare Cancer 1951, 63, 75, 87, 99 South

Dragon Leo 1952, 64, 76, 88, 2000 East
Snake Virgo 1953, 65, 77, 89, 2001 North
Horse Libra 1954, 66, 78, 90, 2002 West
Goat Scorpio 1955, 67, 79, 91, 2003 South

Monkey Sagittarius 1956, 68, 80, 92, 2004 East
Rooster Capricorn 1957, 69, 81, 93, 2005 North
Dog Aquarius 1958, 70, 82, 94, 2006 West
Pig/Boar Pisces 1959, 71, 83, 95, 2007 South

(13) The dating of the calendar round used by the Aztecs is well-known. The last pre-Conquest ceremony was held in 1507 in the year 2-Reed. This would make 1923 and 1975 calendar round years. 1975

would have been 9 cycles of 52 since 1507. The Harmonic Convergence of 1987 was set in part because 1987 is 9 cycles of 52 years (468 years) since 1519, the year Cortés set foot in Mexico. These were both 1-Reed years. See Townsend (1979) p.62.

(14) The date of the first of the year moves in a 1,508 year cycle and does not appear to have been fixed in any specific part of the seasonal year. See Edmonson (1988) p.107, 112.

(15) Tedlock (1982) p.100. Durán (1971) p.392.

Footnotes to Chapter 11: **The Cycle of the Thirteen Katuns**

(1) Landa (1978) p.82.

(2) Sun/Venus conjunctions, both superior and inferior, only occur in five sections of the zodiac spaced apart by 1/5 of the circle or about 72 degrees. This is the quintile aspect in Western astrology. These conjunction points, listed in Appendix C, precess over time covering 72 degrees in roughly the same length of time as the cycle of 13 katuns. The full cycle of Sun/Venus conjunction precession takes approximately 1231 years.

REFERENCES

Arguelles, Jose A.
1984. *Earth Ascending*. Boulder: Shambhala.
1987. *The Mayan Factor*. Santa Fe: Bear and Company.

Aveni, Anthony F.
1975. ed. *Archaeoastronomy in Pre-Columbian America*. Austin: University of Texas Press.
1977. ed. *Native American Astronomy*. Austin: University of Texas Press.
1980. *Skywatchers of Ancient Mexico*. Austin: University of Texas Press.
1989. *Empires of Time: Calendars, Clocks, and Cultures*. New York: Basic Books.
1992. *Conversing with the Planets*. New York: Times Books.
1992. ed. *The Sky in Mayan Literature*. New York: Oxford University Press.

Bierhorst, John.
1990. *The Mythology of Mexico and Central America*. New York: William Morrow and Company, Inc.

Bricker, Harvey and Victoria Bricker.
1992. "Zodiacal References in the Maya Codices." In *The Sky in Mayan Literature*. ed. Anthony Aveni. New York: Oxford University Press.

Brotherston, Gordon.
1979. *Image of the New World: The American Continent Portrayed in Native Texts*. London: Thames and Hudson.

Brundage, Burr Cartwright.
1981. *The Phoenix of the Western World: Quetzalcoatl and the Sky Religion.* Norman, Oklahoma: University of Oklahoma Press.

Burland, C.A.
1967. *The Gods of Mexico.* New York: G.P.Putnam's Sons.

Carlson, John B.
1981. "Numerology and the Astronomy of the Maya." In *Archaeoastronomy in the Americas,* edited by Ray A. Williamson, pp.205-213. Los Altos, CA: Ballena Press.
1991. *Venus-Regulated Warfare and Ritual Sacrifice in Mesoamerica: Teotihuacan and the Cacaxtla "Star Wars" Connection.* College Park, Maryland: The Center for Archaeoastronomy.

Carrasco, David.
1982. *Quetzalcoatl and the Irony of Empire.* Chicago: University of Chicago Press.
1990. *Religions of Mesoamerica.* New York: Harper and Row.
Caso, Alfonso.
1967. *Los Calendarios Prehispanicos.* Mexico: Universidad Nacional Autonoma de Mexico.

Casteneda, Carlos.
1974. *Tales of Power.* New York: Simon and Schuster.

Codex Perez and the Book of Chilam Balam of Mani.
1979. Trans. by Eugene R. Craine and Reginal C. Reindorp. Norman: University of Oklahoma Press.

Codice Chimalpopoca.
1975. Mexico: Universidad Nacional.

Coe, Michael D.
1962. *Mexico.* Mexico, D.F.: Ediciones Lara.
1968. *America's First Civilization.* New York: American Heritage Publishing Co.

Cook de Leonard, Carmen.
1975. "A New Astronomical Interpretation of the Four Ballcourt Panels at Tajin, Mexico." In *Archaeostronomy in Pre-Columbian America,* ed. A. Aveni. Austin, TX: University of Texas Press.

1976. ed., *Esplendor del Mexica Antigua.* 2 vols. Mexico, D.F., Editorial del Valle de Mexico.

Davies, Nigel.
1973. *The Aztecs.* London: Abacus.
1982. *The Ancient Kingdoms of Mexico.* New York: Penguin Books

Del Castillo, Bernal Díaz.
1956.(1601) *The Discovery and Conquest of Mexico.* Trans. by A.P. Maudslay. New York: Farrar, Strauss and Cudahy.

Díaz, Gisele and Alan Rodgers.
1993. *The Codex Borgia.* New York: Dover Publications.

Durán, Fray Diego.
1971. *The Book of the Gods and the Rites and the Ancient Calendar.* Trans. and ed. by F. Horcasitas and D. Heyden. Norman: University of Oklahoma Press.

Edmonson, Munro S.
1988. *The Book of the Year: Middle American Calendar Systems.* Salt Lake City: University of Utah Press.

Furst, Jill Leslie.
1978. *Codex Vindobonensis.* Albany NY: Institute for Mesoamerican Studies.

Gutierrez, Arturo Meza.
1987. *El Calendario de Mexico.* Mexico, D.F.: Kapulli Toltekayotl.
Hay, Clarence L., Ralph Linton, Samuel K. Lothrop, Harry L Shapiro, editors.

1977. *The Maya and Their Neighbors.* Essays on Middle American Anthropology and Archaeology. New York: Dover Publications.

Jenkins, John Major.
1992. *Tzolkin: Visonary Perspectives and Calendar Studies.* Boulder, Colorado: Four Ahau Press.

Kelly, David H.
1980. "Astronomical Identities of Mesoamerican Gods." In *Archaeoastronomy,* no.2, College Park, MD.

Knight, John Alden.
1972. *Moon Up, Moon Down.* Montoursville, PA: Solunar Sales.

Krupp, Dr. E.C.
1978. *In Search of Ancient Astronomies.* New York: McGraw Hill.
1983. *Echoes of the Ancient Skies.* New York: Harper and Row.

Landa, Friar Diego de.
1978. *Yucatan Before and After the Conquest.* Trans. William Gates. New York: Dover Publications.

Leon-Portilla, Miguel.
1963. *Aztec Thought and Culture.* Norman: University of Oklahoma Press.
1969. *Pre-Columbian Literatures of Mexico.* Norman: University of Oklahoma Press.
1973. *Time and Reality in the Thought of the Maya.* Trans. C.L. Boiles and F. Horcasitas. Boston: Beacon Press.
1980. ed. *Native Mesoamerican Spirituality.* New York: Paulist Press.

Luce, Gay Gaer.
1971. *Biological Rhythms in Human and Animal Physiology.* New York: Dover Publications.

Makemsom, Maud W.
1951. *The Book of the Jaguar Priest: A Translation of the Book of Chilam Balam of Tizimin, with Commentary.* New York: Henry Schuman.

Marin, Carlos Martinez.
1961. *Codice Laud.* Mexico: Instituto Nacional de Antropologia e Historia.

Markman, Roberta H. and Peter T. Markman.
1992. *The Flayed God: The Mesoamerican Mythological Tradition.* San Francisco: Harper.

Men, Hunbatz.
1990. *Secrets of Mayan Science/Religion.* Santa Fe: Bear and Co.

Morley, Sylvanus Griswold. 1956. *The Ancient Maya.* Stanford: Stanford University Press.
1975. *An Introduction to the Study of Maya Heiroglyphs.* New York: Dover Publications.

Neugebauer, O.
1957. *The Exact Sciences in Antiquity.* Reprinted in 1969, New York: Dover Publications.

Nuttall, Zelia.
1975. ed. *Codex Nuttall: A Picture Manuscript from Ancient Mexico.* New York: Dover.

Paddock, John, ed.
1966. *Ancient Oaxaca.* Stanford CA: Stanford University Press.

Prescott, William H.
1863. *History of the Conquest of Mexico.* New York: The Modern Library.

Roys, R. L.
1967. *The Book of Chilam Balam of Chumayel.* Norman: University of Oklahoma Press.

Rudhyar, Dane.
1976. *An Astrological Study of Psychological Complexes.* Berkeley, CA: Shambhala.

Sahagún, Fray Bernardino de.
1957. *Florentine Codex: General History of the Things of New Spain, Books 4 and 5.* Trans. C.E. Dibble and A.J.O. Anderson. Ogden: University of Utah Press.

Schele, Linda and David Freidel.
1990. *A Forest of Kings: The Untold Story of the Ancient Maya.* New York: William Morrow and Company.
1993. (with Joy Parker) *Maya Cosmos: Three Thousand Years on the Shaman's Path.* New York: William Morrow and Company.

Schultz, Joachim.
1986. *Movement and Rhythms of the Stars.* Spring Valley, NY: Floris Books/Anthroposophic Press.

Seler, Eduard.
1901. *The Tonalamatl of the Aubin Collection.* Berlin and London.
1901-1902. *Codex Fejervary-Mayer: An Old Mexican Picture Manuscript in the Liverpool Free Public Museum.* Trans. A.H. Keane. Berlin and London.
1902-1903. *Codex Vaticanus B.* Berlin and London.

Stevens, John L.
1843. *Incidents of Travel in Yucatan.* 2 vols. New York: Harper. (Reprinted by Dover Publications, New York, 1961)

Tedlock, Barbara.
1982. *Time and the Highland Maya.* Albuquerque: University of New Mexico Press.

Tedlock, Dennis.
1985. *Popol Vuh*. New York: Simon and Schuster.

Thompson, J.Eric S.
1966. *The Rise and Fall of Maya Civilization*. Norman: University of Oklahoma Press.
1960. *Maya Hieroglyphic Writing: An Introduction*. Norman: University of Oklahoma Press.
1970. *Maya History and Religion*. Norman: University of Oklahoma Press.
1972. *Commentary on the Dresden Codex*. Philadelphia: The American Philosophical Society.

Tompkins, Peter.
1976. *Mysteries of the Mexican Pyramids*. New York: Harper and Row.

Tompkins, Ptolemy.
1990. *This Tree Grows Out of Hell*. San Francisco: Harper.

Torres, Yolotl Gonzalez.
1979. *El Culto a los Astros Entre los Mexicas*. Mexico: Sep Diana.

Tunnicliffe, K.C.
1979. *Aztec Astrology*. Essex: L.N. Fowler and Co. Ltd.

Van Zantwijk, Rudolph.
1985. *The Aztec Arrangement*. Norman, OK: University of Oklahoma Press.

Van der Waerden, Bartel.
1974. *Science Awakening II, The Birth of Astronomy*. New York: Oxford University Press.

Volguine, Alexandre.
1969. *Astrology of the Mayas and Aztecs*. Kent, England: Pythago-

rean Publications.

Waters, Frank.
1975. *Mexico Mystique: The Coming Sixth World of Consciousness.*
Chicago: Swallow Press.

Williamson, Ray A.
1981. ed. *Archaeoastronomy in the Americas.* Los Altos, California:
Ballena Press and College Park, Maryland: Center for Archaeoastronomy.

Willson, Robert W.
1924. "Astronomical Notes on the Maya Codices." In *Papers of the
Peabody Museum of American Archaeology and Ethnology,
Harvard University.* Cambridge, MA: Peabody Museum, Harvard
University.

Zerubavel, Eviatar. 1983. *The Seven Day Circle: The History and
Meaning of the Week.* Chicago: University of Chicago Press.